THE BOOK OF
NUMEROLOGY
TAKING A COUNT OF YOUR LIFE

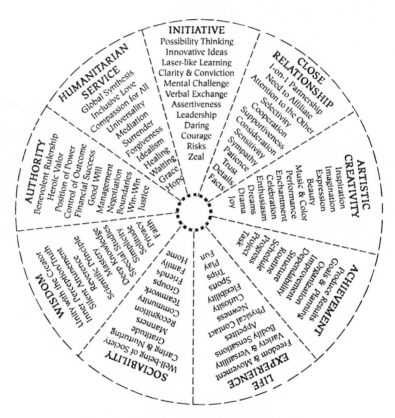

Spectrum of the Nine Living Harmonies

THE BOOK OF NUMEROLOGY
TAKING A COUNT OF YOUR LIFE

Hal A. Lingerman

SAMUEL WEISER, INC.

York Beach, Maine

First published in 1994 by
Samuel Weiser, Inc.
P. O. Box 612
York Beach, ME 03910–0612

Library of Congress Cataloging-in-Publication Data

Lingerman, Hal A.
    The book of numerology : taking a count of your life /
  by Hal A. Lingerman.
        p.   cm.
    Includes bibliographical references and index.
    1. Symbolism of numbers.   2. Spiritual life.   I. Title.
  BF1623.P9L566   1994
    133.3'35—dc20   94–16826
ISBN 0–87728–804–6   CIP
BJ

Cover illustration is titled *Spirale zum Jenseits* (Spiral).
Copyright © 1994 Klaus Holitzka. Used by permission of
the Walter Holl Agency, Germany.

Printed in the United States of America

99 98
10 9 8 7 6 5 4 3 2

Typeset in 11 point Palatino

The paper used in this publication meets the minimum
requirements of the American National Standard for
Permanence of Paper for Printed Library Materials
Z39.48–1984.

TABLE OF CONTENTS

Part III: Counseling and Numerics

PREFACE

Real imagination is the spiritual harmony of
countless diversities. Imagination calls forth the
images of something divine which animates all
things.   —Eleanor C. Merry[1]

When you are able to blend completely with all
things, then you are truly part of the whole.
                                              —Sun Bear[2]

As a person, you are a multidimensional being: a complex
and creative organism. Through your own soul and temperament, you are expressing the glory of the Creator. Your
temperament is composed of the personality vehicles that
you are refining by your own consciousness and choices.
The vehicles of your outer personality are moving at different frequencies of consciousness. These frequencies and
interacting harmonies of your physical body, your emotions, your mind, and intuitive faculties are always changing. They are composed of the various essences, atoms,
memories, abilities and challenges that you are born to
refine and integrate during this lifetime. Thus, ultimately
there is no blame: you are here to become all that you are
created to be: increasingly, progressively beautiful and
complete in the Love of God.

Every person's life is valuable—in itself and as a part
of the greater totality. At any moment every one of us can
reveal incredible gifts, potencies, and constructive capacities. New therapeutic approaches today are mining
untapped resources and opportunities for renewal in each
of us. We are discovering powerful, creative energies in the
universe that can motivate us and direct us, from within
ourselves, toward more healing outcomes.

---

[1]Eleanor C. Merry, *Art: Its Occult Basis and Healing Value* (East Grinstad, Sussex,
England: New Knowledge Books, 1961), p. 104.
[2]Sun Bear, *The Medicine Wheel* (Englewood Cliffs, NJ: Prentice-Hall, 1987), p. 4.

We are discovering new ways to care for ourselves and for each other. We are becoming more fully alive. We are opening new doors into all of our relationships by expanding the expression of our physical, emotional, mental and intuitive-spiritual faculties. We can learn to:

Experience recovery and a more balanced release of our physical addictions and primitive, abusive, aggressive behaviors.

Find greater self-worth and new outlets for nurturing and friendship as we accept and cope with long and deeply buried emotional hurts and numbed feelings.

Move toward a more educated clarity that dissolves fear, competition, controlling will, denial, mental rigidity, prejudice, and judgmental opinions.

Contact inner resources of inspiration and realize in ourselves a luminous guidance that is available directly from the Infinite as our intuitive-spiritual perception expands and outgrows religious dogma.

Increasing attitudes of cooperation and synthesis are awakening greater mutual respect and power. Greater networking provides results that can be win-win, bringing further opportunities for bonding, healing and transformation. Each one of us is here to contribute the best of who we are to the greater totality and wholeness. We are all interconnected. Amid differences of age, culture, religion, language, temperament and past experience, we can yet identify common ground. By coming to know and give ourselves, we can help to open new horizons of acceptance, healing, caring and compassionate love for all that lives.

ACKNOWLEDGMENTS

The Book of Numerology is a companion to the book *Living Your Destiny* (Samuel Weiser, York Beach, Maine, 1992). This work is the result of more than twenty years of research and testing, based upon my interactions with many persons that I have met in university teaching, counseling, and ministry.

The Book of Numerology is a practical manual for life direction, which can be used by counselors, teachers, administrators, and many other professionals. In its own way, this book is a clear indicator of each person's life journey and can be used by any person, of any age or culture.

I thank the many persons who have helped to make this book possible, especially the following:

The Reverend Flower A. Newhouse, Christian mystic, spiritual teacher and friend, who instructed me in different aspects of the Pythagorean Triangle and encouraged me to study and investigate further in spiritual understanding. Reverend Newhouse is the founder of The Questhaven Retreat, located in Escondido, California.

Dr. Juno Jordan, dentist, esoteric teacher and numerologist, who at the age of 95, kindly spent valuable hours teaching me the finer points of numbers in her home in Santa Monica.

Dr. Ernest Wilson, Unity minister, author, teacher and friend, who in 1973 first introduced me to the science of numbers.

Judy Mathes, extraordinary teacher, author, and friend, who so carefully helped me to prepare this manuscript for publication, and tirelessly encouraged me along the way.

Rosemary and Aria, my wonderful wife and daughter, and my mother, Millie, who are a continuous source of joy and wonder in my life.

With appreciation for these and others' many kindnesses and insights, I humbly offer this book, hoping that it may be beneficial and spiritually inspiring to all sincere seekers on the Path leading Godward.

Ring out ye Crystal spheres,
Once bless our human ears. . .
And let your silver chime
Move in melodious time. . .
And with your ninefold harmony,
Make up full consort to the Angelic symphony.

—John Milton
"On the Morning of Christ's Nativity"

INTRODUCTION

That I might finish my course with joy
(Acts 20:24).

I have glorified thee on the earth:
I have finished the work which thou gave me to do
(John 17:4).[1]

THE CHANCE OF A LIFETIME! Like a painter's canvas waiting to be filled, your life journey awaits you. With the palette of your soul's experience, how will you bring form and color to the picture of your present lifetime? Many opportunities call you forward, and you are a distinct individual, with your own unique talents, potentialities, and challenges. As the brilliant scientist and educator, Dr. Alfred Tomatis, points out, the possibilities for your advancement and spiritual progress are limitless:

> You are never limited by what you appear to be. There exists within you all sorts of possibilities which allow you to surpass yourself again and again.[2]

In the miracle of new birth and entry into this lifetime, each of us has come through a careful preparation in the inner worlds. With the careful help of God's higher helpers, I believe we have chosen the parents and environments best suited to our present needs; we have experienced our time of conception—the months of waiting, watching and feeling as our bodies and predispositions formed in the mother's womb. As the pioneering physician, Dr. Thomas Verny,

---

[1] All biblical quotes are from the King James version.
[2] Alfred A. Tomatis, *The Conscious Ear* (Barrytown, NY: Station Hill Press, 1991), p. 15.

points out in his excellent book, *The Secret Life of the Unborn Child*,

> The womb, in a very real sense, establishes the child's expectations. If it has been a warm, loving environment, the child is likely to expect the outside world to be the same. This produces a predisposition toward trust, openness, extroversion and self-confidence. The world will be his oyster, just as the womb has been.
>
> If that environment has been hostile, the child will anticipate that his new world will be equally uninviting. He [she] will be predisposed toward suspiciousness, distrust and introversion. Relating to others will be hard, and so will self-assertion. Life will be more difficult for him [her] than for a child who had a good womb experience.[3]

At our appointed time we arrived at the gates of birth, and we entered this earthly lifetime, totally vulnerable to whatever reception and environment greeted us. Thus, the developmental stages of our life journey began. How wonderful in this time of history, that scientific, psychological, and spiritual discoveries help us to view our life with a clearer sense of purpose. We now recognize definite needs and desires that are crucial to specific stages of our journey. In the midst of our free will, an increasing wisdom informs our choices, so that we need not always fumble blindly or proceed just by chance. As each generation identifies its needs, sensitivity increases. We are better able to break with the past and its self-defeating chains of repeated ignorance and pain. We can change our ways! We can learn how to give what we may have needed but never received. In

---

[3]Thomas Verny, *The Secret Life of the Unborn Child* (New York, NY: Dell, 1981), p. 50.

this manner, our children, who come through us into this lifetime, will receive a greater sense of welcome; they will experience feelings of being wanted, loved and acknowledged for their needs and for who they truly are. Perhaps, for the first time in history, the love and wisdom emanating from the heavens can stream into the womb experience, flowing through the gates of birth into the responsive environment of parents and home. In this way every incoming life will begin with greater hope, respect, bonding, and the kind of warm welcome that will provide the ingredients and understanding most needed for genuine child development and soul enrichment.

In this book we will look at ways to identify the specific needs of each individual. Whether we are children or adults, we experience various cycles of opportunity and challenge. The more each person's needs and basic temperament can be described, the more clearly we can suggest various choices and options that may be helpful. Many approaches for understanding each person have been suggested through the years. In our time we can observe a growing synthesis of various psychological and spiritual disciplines, including the concepts of the great thinker Pythagoras, and others who perceived each person as a living constellation of expanding energies and frequencies. To describe each person's capacities for response, Pythagoras suggested an inner mathematics that paints a moving picture of how different energies in each person are interacting and producing specific results. In the spirit of Pythagoras, we can thus learn to view each person as an energy field, embodying the great energies of the universe. Various questions such as, "Why did I choose my particular parents and place of birth?" or "What are my abilities?" or "What are my major needs and desires this lifetime?" or "What lessons do I need to learn?" will yield their very special responses as we draw upon the ideas of Pythagoras and others who have followed in his spirit. In this way, each person's life reveals a fascinating journey—a dance and a moving process. The varied configurations of energy that we are expressing become visible as our particular responses and behaviors. These are produced by our perception and our choices.

In my twenty years of university teaching, counseling and ministry, I have tried, however gropingly, to view each person as a unique, dynamic, ever-changing field of energies, not as a static human being, who is limited by a label, a condemning diagnosis, or a recurring condition. Each person is an individual who emanates from Divinity. We all can express an ever growing creativity and purpose. We can find our dream and focus. I believe each of us holds keys in ourselves that can unlock a virtually unlimited power from the infinite Godhead. When this power is harnessed and directed lovingly toward all others, we truly begin to release God's Light in our life. In our own particular paths of service, we discover a larger fulfillment. Our fears decrease. Our sense of meaning arises from our fuller attunement with the Source of all goodness; we draw creatively upon this immensity of power, and we find our distortions and limitations beginning to move into harmony and balance. We forgive all that has happened, and we move forward. The energy spectrum of our life reveals a variety of themes and interests; our life's painting begins to take shape ever more beautifully on our canvas. Moving in the limitless light of God, with growing love and clear purpose, we proceed into the great Mystery, and we respond joyously as we become more clearly visible and increasingly real to all.

PART I

BASIC NUMEROLOGY

THEMES OF YOUR LIFE

One way of viewing yourself is to see yourself as a living energy field—a garden—that from birth, is growing and continuously being filled with the seeds of your life themes, opportunities, and experiences. Great energies from on high, like laser beams or power lines of light, are vibrating through you, animating you with new currents and offering archetypes for your journey. As a receptor, according to your consciousness, you respond with your antennae of thoughts, feelings, and actions. Power streams of energy contain the thematic materials of your lifetime. These are described, by Pythagoras and others after him in terms of *Number*—an inner mathematics. You can look at your energy field as a dynamic energy spectrum, contained in the numbered essences, **ONE** through **NINE**. The power lines emanating from Divinity, as described in these nine primary numerical energies, are like currents charging you and inspiring you to become God's fuller expression of abundant life.

These nine primary energy currents, accessible to all persons as *Number*, are thoroughly described in my book, *Living Your Destiny* (Samuel Weiser, York Beach, Maine, 1992). These nine power streams, with their particular themes and focus, circulate through our physical, emotional, mental, and intuitive consciousness and correspond to the nine basic themes of life.

The Nine Power Streams

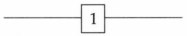

Autonomy, possibility thinking, pioneer concepts, verbal stimulation, independence, courage, and learning to assert oneself mentally and physically by leading the way. God's providence supplies many openings.

Practicality, trust, close bonding, consideration, emotional affiliation, and intimate partnership; building security and emotional safety by forming bridges of communication; being supportive to the other person's needs, often by providing the necessary information, data, and details.

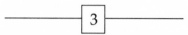

Creativity, inspiration, and artistic self-expression; beauty and imagination, the inner world of dreams and reverie, joy, romance, and Nature.

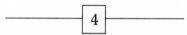

Purposeful achievement through work, structured tasks, and planned projects; being dependable in labor and producing useful outcomes based upon goals and objectives; intense and thorough effort; steadfastness and follow-through.

Freedom in motion, sensations, newness, and physical vitality; making personal contacts, coordinating many variables, adapting to sudden changes while remaining centered in the moment; finding visceral release through the physical body, often in exercise, sports, and travel; maintaining physical health in the midst of strong drives and appetites; bringing love into physical contact.

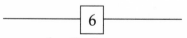

Service to the group: family, home, peers and community; caring and friendship, loving and being loved, helping to nurture others; serving society, primarily in areas of teaching, counseling, entertainment and community services.

Spirituality and deepening attunement to the Infinite; penetrating the great Mystery by gaining self-understanding and specialized knowledge through study, research, and investigation; finding meaning in life through quiet observation and inner reflection.

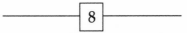

Success through power, authority and management; strong use of will-power; rules and empowers others with benevolence; win-win outcomes arise from firm policy, negotiation, and clear boundaries; strong supervision and good stewardship improve investments, finances and yield profitable outcomes.

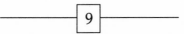

Universal brotherhood and compassion, peace, forgiveness and reconciliation; tying up loose ends and paying off old debts; maintaining vision and high ideals in the midst of limitations, interferences, and delays; bringing hope and working for the greater good of the totality.

What Your Birthdate Tells You

Your birthdate describes the spectrum of energies, capabilities, and challenges that you brought into this lifetime. You cannot change your birthdate! Its energies describe converging streams of cosmic power that are circulating through you. Certain proportions and combinations of these energies are unique to your life. They suggest specific areas of talent and creativity, potentials for character building, and possible fields of service and employment. In addition, the particular intensities of energy that flow through you will show you areas of your life that may bring challenges and may need balancing and integration. You will see how to modify or bring forward some areas of your life, while tempering and diversifying others. You will find new ways to express your relationships with others. You will discover many varied facets of your total being, all capable of growing into finer harmonies of expression.

Your Birthdate and the Pythagorean Triangle

It is important to identify how different energies in you are mingling and interacting. All the energies are potentially helpful to your larger life expression. Try not to fixate upon just one energy stream or any single numerical tone of your temperament while losing sight of the larger totality. (Example: avoid saying, "I am a THREE"; try to see how the more dominant energy of THREE interacts with the other numbers of the triangle.) The Pythagorean triangle is a way to work toward integration; its contents will give you clues about how various streams of energy (different numbers ONE through NINE) can blend together in you. As in music, it is important to learn how to harmonize various notes or energies in yourself, so that different chords or tones of expression may sound forth more clearly.[1]

To put your birthdate into a Pythagorean triangle, begin by writing your birthdate in numbers. For example,

---

[1]See also, Juno Jordan, *Numerology: The Romance of Your Name* (Santa Barbara, CA: J. F. Rowny Press, 1965).

March 23, 1986 would be written as 3 23 19 86. Leave sufficient space between the numbers of the month, day and year. Now draw a triangle around your birthdate as shown in figure 1 below.

Reduce each of the four numerical energies (the numbers of the day, month, and year) in the triangle to *single* digit numbers by adding the digits of the numerical energies greater than 10 together. For example, the numerical energy 10 reduces to **1** because 1 + 0 = 1. Therefore, if your month of birth is October (10), the reduced numerical energy is **1** (1 + 0 = 1); if your month of birth is November (11) the reduced numerical energy is **2** (1 + 1 = 2); if your month of birth is December (12) the reduced numerical energy is **3** (1 + 2 = 3); and so on.

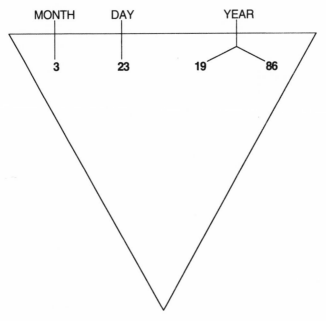

Figure 1. An example of the birthdate March 23, 1986 placed in a Pythagorean triangle.

If you find that once two digits of a numerical energy are added together the sum is 10 or greater than 10, simply add the digits of the new sum together. For example, if you were born in 1968 the numerical energies of 19 and 68 (the birth year broken into two numbers) would break down as **1** (1 + 9 = 10 which in turn breaks down to 1 + 0 = **1**) and **5** (6 + 8 = 14 which in turn breaks down to 1 + 4 = **5**).

Once you have figured out each of the four numerical energies in your Pythagorean triangle write the number below the original birthdate numbers. For an example of how this should look, see figure 2 below.

Continue to bring the columns of the numerical energies down the triangle by adding the numerical energy of columns 1 and 2 (month and day) and the numerical ener-

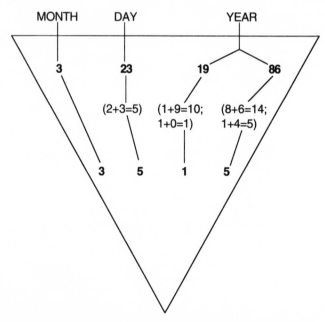

Figure 2. The numerical energies of the birthdate March 23, 1986 reduced to single digits.

gy of columns 3 and 4 (the two numbers that make up the year of birth). Again, if the sums are 10 or greater, reduce to one digit by adding the two numbers together. Complete the energy spectrum of your triangle by adding the final two numbers together. If necessary, reduce to a number less than 10. For an example of a completed Pythagorean triangle, see figure 3 below.

Once you have reached a single number at the bottom of the triangle, you have now gathered together the energy spectrum of your Pythagorean triangle. Pythagoras called this triangle the Holy Tetraktys, that which contains and describes the creative interplay of the energies present in each person's life.

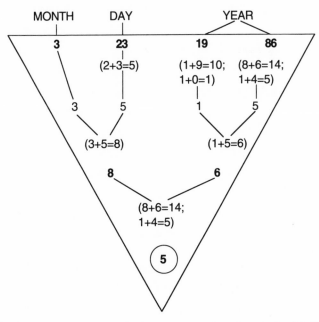

Figure 3. A completed Pythagorean triangle of the birthdate March 23, 1986.

Interpreting Your Triangle

You are now ready to interpret the numerical energies, as they are moving together within your energy field, as described by the numbers in your triangle. *Remember, all numbers, as energies, are potentially good,* especially as you learn how to work with them. Try to see these energies as dynamic forces within you, vibrating, dancing and interacting in your life. To gain fuller understanding of the positions and proportions of these forces, keep in mind the following components of your energy field:

▼ Birth Force Energy: The final number, at the base of your triangle. (This is your strongest energy.)

▼ Day of Birth Energy: Another powerful, secondary energy that needs to be harmonized with the Birth Force energy.

▼ Dominant Energy: Numbers present in large quantities within the triangle.

▼ Recessive Energy: "Missing" numbers within the triangle that usually require more effort to contact and bring forward. (Occasionally, such numbers represent energies previously developed.)

▼ Juxtapositions: How various numerical energies are interacting.

▼ Tonalities: The "keyboard" of energy currents; proportions denoted by how the *quantity* (how many of a certain number is in the triangle) of each energy *blends with the essence* (the particular numerical energy itself) of each number. (Example: three 5's = 5:3)

▼ Cycles: Specific periods of time when certain energies are emphasized in our life, thus offering a certain focus for opportunity and change.

BIRTH FORCE ENERGY

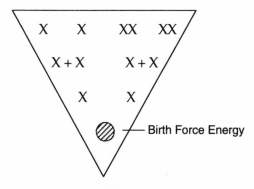

Your Birth Force Energy is the final numerical energy located at the base of your triangle. This is the strongest energy in your constellation, and all the other energies funnel down into this central numerical intensity. Thus, the Birth Force Energy represents the primary influence, at the center of all the other energies that appear in your triangle. In your birth force number, you can identify many of your primary motivations, needs, and responses.

Basic Interpretations

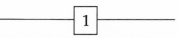

Mentally you are very independent, direct, eager and quick to discover new ideas and new possibilities. Your pioneering ventures reach ahead to create the future. You want autonomy in your life and work—the room and freedom to think your thoughts and to express your views verbally and openly. Your mind demands continuous new inputs and challenges. You are a catalyst wherever you go. You think for yourself. Your views are often different; your vision is daring. You take the lead. Often you may "shoot from the hip" verbally.

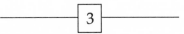

Emotionally, you desire safety and close bonding with another person or with something that gives you feelings of security through participation and affiliation. You enjoy intimacy, and you need to be needed. You prefer to be supportive more than to be in the lead. You want all the particulars—facts, details, and data—and you are intrigued by intricacies. You do best when someone whom you trust is encouraging you. You do not like to be rushed. You tend to take things personally. You are interested in the golden moments of life that we sometimes call "cameos." Basically, you are very subjective and selective: you either link quickly with someone emotionally or you don't. As you develop confidence, you become less dependent, and a more agreeable partner in a relationship. Information replaces fears and vacant hopes.

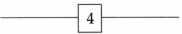

Emotionally, you are motivated by your dreams and imagination. You are very creative and artistic. You enjoy life's beautiful moments. You thrive on romance and enchantment. Much of your life is likely to be lived "on the wing" in the moment of rapture. A part of you does not like too much structure. You can be quite dramatic, perhaps even histrionic, enjoying the grand gesture. In difficult times you can "space out" easily, going into your own world of creativity, fantasy, and imagination. Your powers of visualization allow you to see it, dream it, feel it, and express it.

Physically, you are a hard worker, who enjoys achievement and accomplishment. A part of you likes structure and routine. You are a good planner, and you get the job done thoroughly. You are steadfast and very dependable, the "salt of the earth" and the pillar of strength on which many others might lean. You get so much done in a day that others may see you as an intense, tireless "whirlwind of energy." You usually have tasks or projects going on all around you. You finish what you start. You are purposeful and reliable.

5

Physically, you enjoy variety, newness and sensation. Much of your life is lived in motion, and you want freedom to explore and to experience new adventures. Travel stimulates your interests and curiosity. Excitement and frequent, sudden changes fill your life. Your capacity to be flexible and adaptable, but sometimes outrageous, relieves many of your tensions and irritations. You do best with wide open spaces and room to move. You can find new ways to care for your body and to express your appetites and pleasures with some moderation and good sense. In the midst of many changing interests, you can still finish some of the things you've started. You can be bold without arguing or agitating. You can get attention without being crude or obnoxious. Humor relieves life's pressures. You can be a good referee who knows how to "roll with the punches." You can handle many options and sudden changes.

6

You are emotionally nourished by friendships and social interactions. Your primary emotional focus comes from you home, family, peers, and community. You are a helper to others, and you have abilities as a teacher, counselor and entertainer. If you feel good about yourself, you can make others feel good. You enjoy having others around you, and your social calendar is usually full. Your caring and kindness can do much to add to the well-being of people, animals, nature, and society. Status and appreciation mean much to you, but you attract more genuine friends when you are true to yourself and to your values. You often enjoy nurturing others, especially the underdog and the outcast.

You are interested in the deeper mysteries of life. You enjoy specialized study, and you are continuously learning. In quiet reflection and solitude, you make your own inner connection with your Creator. You are likely to pursue deeper areas of investigation, such as metaphysics, psychology or science. Even if you don't say much, when you do speak, it counts. In many ways you may live outside the mainstream; your times alone, in meditation, replenish you and bring you insight. You live best out of your own inner centeredness and intuitive focus. A side of you is very private. You are also a good researcher. You analyze a situation with clarity and depth.

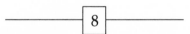

A large part of you wants to be in charge, wielding the power and authority. You have the abilities to manage and supervise. You desire success, and you enjoy giving the orders, while others may work hard to carry them out. Money is important to you. Control is also a major theme in your life. Your will is very strong, and you aim to enforce and complete whatever you start. By setting limits and establishing policies, you take good care of property and investments. You empower others with your own power. Remembering your sense of justice and fairness, you overcome bossiness and domination. In your negotiations, you make your outcomes a win-win for others. Your benevolence makes you less coercive.

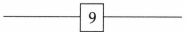

Your essential nature is strongly humanitarian and inclusive. Through service to all cultures and races of people, you find your own identity and place in the Creator's plan. You can see the best in people and conditions, even though many times in life you cannot control outer circumstances. Attitudes of forgiveness and compassion bring out the best in you, and your altruistic ways open many doors. Keep moving ahead; do not get stuck in the past or in others' behaviors or misfortunes. Bring hope and help where you can, but avoid unnecessary martyrdom. Infinite Grace and an unconditional Love uphold you in difficult times. You can see the "big picture," and the panoramic view. Your vision inspires others. You can work towards transformation by rising above disappointments and by seeing new alternatives. You can always look for the open door. Like Prometheus, you can break the chains of confinement. Even in the midst of outer difficulties and hindrances, by persisting with hope, you will experience eventual breakthroughs in your circumstances.

DAY OF BIRTH ENERGY

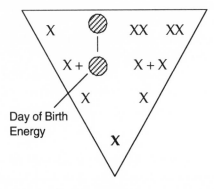

Your Day of Birth Energy describes a secondary numerical energy that can be an important ally with your Birth Force Energy. Try to integrate these two primary energies. Harmonize these two forces within yourself so that they can work together instead of being at odds with each other. For example, a 5 Birth Force Energy (indicating a strong need for freedom, movement, physical sensation, excitement, and flexibility) could work well with a 4 Day of Birth Energy (which indicates a need for structure, task, planning, routine, and achievement). If these two sides of yourself cooperate and allow time for each other, you will find balance. Freedom needs some structure and follow-through, so this underpinning provides the stability for acceptable play time to occur. Thus, work and play, structure and spontaneity, dependability and flexibility, and other 4/5 energies in combination are like alternating currents that can be brought together in creative and constructive rhythms. If the energies of the Birth Force and Day of Birth are the same, then that energy is squared and greatly magnified.

In summary, identify the Birth Force Number and the Day of Birth Number. Find ways to integrate both of these energies in your make-up so that they do not conflict with each other. Allow each energy its own rightful time in your life expression.

Basic Interpretations

You have a strong independent streak. You think for your-self, and, at times, you may be reluctant to listen to others' thinking. A part of you wants to do it your own way and you want others to listen to you. You may have a difficult time taking direction and correction. Learn how to blend with others better and meet their needs on their terms. When you are trusted, others will listen to your original ideas, be pliable, and learn how to be needed.

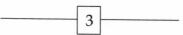

A part of you is more cautious, and you may be quite liter-al, even taking some things very personally. This part of you is also very particular and emotionally demanding. You may have certain fears and worries. You can work through these by getting more information. Express your-self creatively; don't just take in others' energies. Be confi-dent in your own impressions and express your sympa-thies. Be with the person that you can trust deeply and inti-mately. Learn how to be close without leaning too hard or smothering the other.

A part of you is very creative and expressive. Cultivate some artistic outlet that stirs your imagination. There may be times, especially if they are painful ones, when you pre-fer to float over the conflict. Maintain focus in the midst of your flights of fancy. Avoid histrionics and get on with the work at hand. Follow your dream!

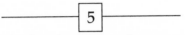

You want to be a dependable achiever, who produces concrete results. You are purposeful and quite steady. Remember to have some fun in the midst of hard work. Overcome rigidity by being able to be flexible if sudden changes occur. Do not do everyone else's work for them. Organize the pieces of your life. Watch your health. Remember to rest *and* play.

A certain amount of excitement and many sudden changes seem to fill your life. What happens isn't always what you expected, but life is never dull. You can adapt well in the moment, rebounding quickly and moving on to the next experience. You may be somewhat of a taster, not always committing yourself for work or lasting relationships. Balance your thirst for sensation and adventure with the ability to contribute meaningfully to society and friends. Make peace with family members. Enjoy life without being radical or excessive in your appetites. Keep within the limits of your own energy field.

Part of you is very much connected to your home and family, as well as friends and peers. You enjoy the company of others, and you may attend many parties and social functions. You are a good entertainer, and your kindness is very helpful to others. Remember to be yourself with all people. Avoid the "chameleon" tendency to please others, telling them only what they want to hear. You do not have to bear the burdens of everyone; even though you do your best, not everyone may like you or appreciate you. Avoid "playing the game" in order to gain status. Become free from enmeshment. Take time to discover yourself.

Part of you is very private and reserved. A certain perfectionism is evident in some of your behaviors and responses. You may be inclined to hold back at times, preferring to maintain your space and a necessary distance. You conserve your energy for study and reflection. You are a very perceptive, accurate observer. You like to live life in a way that yields meaning. You are not content just "doing" or keeping busy. Whatever interests you is something you will investigate thoroughly.

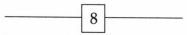

You like to make your own decisions, and you do not like to be told what to do. You like to have the final say, and often think that others should obey your commands. You wield power, and you can be a good manager. You state your limits clearly; you have a strong will, and you want to win. Money is important to you. Know when to set boundaries. Rise above condemnation or vengeful intentions. Work for justice and fair play.

You may find yourself working to realize your ideals in the midst of interferences and delays. You can see the possibilities for harmony and synthesis, even when many factions may be in disagreement. You can mediate for the good of the totality. You see with expansive vision. Find the openings that connect you with service to others, and remain ready and alert as your good comes to you. You attract much love and many unexpected changes. The attitude of compassionate service brings eventual transformation. Keep on keeping on.

DOMINANT ENERGIES

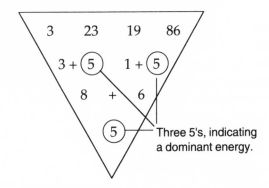

Three 5's, indicating a dominant energy.

Numbers that occur in your triangle more than twice indicate a more dominant energy. Three or more of a certain number indicate a strong concentration of power in a specific area, which naturally needs more outlets for appropriate, creative expression. Try to see how such intensities of energy might be able to combine constructively with other strong energies in your spectrum. For example, several 3s with 5s might indicate a relationship between arts and body, such as dance, body movement, pottery, woodwork, fashion, photographic journalism, bodywork, or travel. Make the intuitive connections that link and strengthen various areas of power within yourself. An integration of several 2s with 6s might show intimacy and partnership with groups, friends, and family activities. Several 4s and 9s may yield constructive results as the task, projects, and labors relate to the needs of humanity.

Basic Interpretations

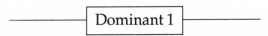

| Dominant 1 |

You have a very active mind; you have many original ideas, and you are likely to be quite verbal. You enjoy being able to express yourself openly and directly. You seek new horizons.

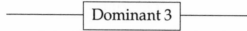

Dominant 2

You are very particular, especially in the ways you handle details and information. At times you may take things very personally, and you may worry excessively, especially about some conditions you cannot change or "fix."

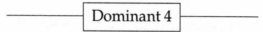

Dominant 3

You have a strong creative side, which needs expressive outlets. Find ways to use your imagination; express yourself in an artistic, dramatic manner.

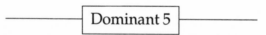

Dominant 4

Your primary focus is on the work and the task. You find structured ways to handle and accomplish projects. You can be very dependable. You like to organize everything.

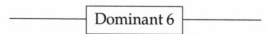

Dominant 5

You may experience many changes in your life. Outer conditions demand that you become flexible and adaptable. You need to move your body and feel life through your senses. You may experience much excitement in your life. Use variety to overcome irritability.

Dominant 6

You probably spend much of your time around people. You have many friends and acquaintances. You help others with your kind and caring ways. Avoid being shamed or trapped in a group. Nurture others, but remember, you deserve appreciation for yourself. Maintain healthy self-esteem.

Dominant 7

You may direct your energies into study and research. Sometimes your life may seem more removed from the outer struggle. You may spend more time alone. Parts of you may be more abstract and private. You aim for depth.

Dominant 8

You can be quite dominant mentally. Much power comes through you in areas of management, authority, supervision, and finances. Empower others with your power.

Dominant 9

You have a large capacity to serve the needs of humanity. You hold many wonderful ideals, and you try a variety of means to further the sense of cooperation and brotherhood. Your compassionate nature reaches into many areas of life.

RECESSIVE ENERGIES

Those numerical energies that are not found in your triangle are called recessive energies. This does *not* mean that you are born deficient or that you lack these energies. Rather, such energies are recessed, much like precious gold buried more deeply in the mine. Thus, with recessive energies, it is often important for you to reach back and dig deeper, in order to uncover and release them. Frequently, the more demanding challenges and crises of your life compel you to discover the hidden layers of power and ability in yourself. And ironically, it is often those difficult areas of your life that you may most need to discover and develop, in order to give them to others who need them. The need activates the hidden talents. Activate and develop what seems to be inaccessible. Find other people who are good in these areas and learn from them. Study lives that have embodied these energies.

As you try to bring forward the missing or recessive numerical energies, try to see just what is recessed and how it relates to other energies that are more immediately evident. For example, a missing 4 energy can be strengthened by the energies of 2, 6, and 8. In other words, the ability to organize (4) can be strengthened by an ability to respond to another's need, to arrange safety in someone's environment, and to get necessary information (2). Similarly, the capacity to be helpful and kind to others (6), and by the use of will-power to complete the assignment successfully (8), will also strengthen a recessive 4 energy.

Basic Interpretations

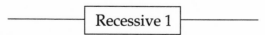

Recessive 1

It is difficult for you to risk. You are a more tentative thinker, who may not find it easy to be direct or innovative.

You may not really know how you think, or you may be afraid to share your thoughts with others. Work on being more assertive and courageous. (–1 will apply only to persons born after 2000 as before the year 2000 it is impossible not to have at least one number 1 when considering your birth data.)

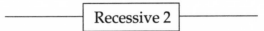

You may be careless about details. You may be emotionally distant. You may lack sympathy. Work on close relationships. Learn how to be supportive of someone else's feelings and needs. You can be more sensitive to your partner.

You may need to develop your creative, artistic abilities. Learn how to express your own talents to a greater degree. Surround yourself with beautiful music, color, poetry, literature, etc. Remember to find joy in your imagination and creative outlets.

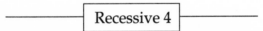

Work on being more dependable. Finish the task and put more routine into your life. Develop goals and take the necessary steps to complete your objectives. Note daily achievements. Plan your day ahead.

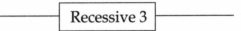

You may need to get more in touch with your body. Listen to your body; take better care of your physical health. Avoid too much excitement and overactivity. Become more flexible to changes. Learn how to relax. Take time to have some fun.

Recessive 6

It may be difficult for you to function in marriage and society, in a domestic environment, or with a group of people. You may need to learn how to blend and conform to certain basic social standards and conventions. Develop better manners, social graces, and the art of friendly chit-chat. Involve yourself as a volunteer in some worthy community project. Maintain your home, family, and friendships. Nurture others more. Overcome feelings of not belonging, low self-esteem, and alienation. Contribute to others' well-being; don't just think of yourself.

Recessive 7

You may lack interior focus and necessary knowledge about yourself, your place in life, your vocation, etc. Work on making a deeper spiritual connection. Through deepened study, quiet reflection, and prayerful contemplation, feel the link with your Creator. See how what you do, feel and think brings its own consequences.

Recessive 8

It may be difficult for you to complete and finish successfully what you have begun. You may not know how to own your own power in a constructive way. Learn more about finances; make the decisions. Follow through. Take charge. Avoid indecisiveness.

Recessive 9

You may need to bring out more feelings of compassion. Try to increase your perspective about a situation or another person. Get a sense of the bigger picture before you make your conclusions. Practice forgiveness. Release the past. Try to see the best in others.

JUXTAPOSITIONS

Juxtapositions of energies in your triangle involve the process of discovering how different energies combine in you and how they can produce the most constructive results. In this area of Pythagorean numerics, you can move from knowledge to intuitive insight. The mysterious comingling and interaction of energies and people bring dynamic outcomes. In this sense no two people need to be "incompatible" if only they can identify and work through their own issues and find ways to interact that are mutually accepting, harmonious, and fulfilling. Even in the midst of personal issues and differing paths in life, an interesting synthesis of approaches can enhance, even transform, the moment. Relationships are thus built upon the following combinations:

Similarities

Both people share the *same* numerical energies with each other, whether odd or even. For example, both people may have a dominance of 1s (independent thinking) and 6s (love of family and group). They can build on each other's strengths.

Complementarities

A couple's energies are both **odd** (1, 3, 5, 7, 9), but each partner's energies are differently **odd** from the other (1, 5, 9 vs. 3, 7). Or, a couple's energies may be more **even** (2, 4, 6, 8), but each individual's energies are differently **even** (4, 6 vs. 2, 8). For example, one person is strong in **3** (creativity, imagination, arts) and **7** (depth of knowledge, research, and inner meditation), and the other partner is strong in **1** (independent thinking and leadership) and **5** (sports and travel).

Opposites

One person has more **odd** numerical energies (1, 3, 5, 7, 9) and the other person has more **even** numerical energies (2, 4, 6, 8). **Odd** breaks up patterns; **even** stabilizes patterns.

If you can move among the nine energy tones with insight and flexibility, no relationships need be impossible or unworkable. Love, awareness, and acceptance must always be present. The flow of certain energies within you can be tempered or redirected, but there cannot be suppression or denial of the basic life energies that are circulating in their varying proportions within each human being. All energies seek their highest expression through you, as your consciousness and your choices magnetize your ability to contact their power.

TONALITIES

Your "tonality keyboard" (a list of how many times each energy, 1–9, appears in your triangle) describes potential talents and reveals opportunities for your life expression.[3] Tonalities of energy describe the relationship between a numerical essence and its quantity in the triangle. Thus, three 5s in your triangle identifies a basic energy current or "energy harmonic" that flows between 3 and 5. Such a vibration indicates a correspondence between the numerical essences of 3 and 5: creativity (3) is relating with the movement of the body and freedom (5). Putting these currents together, we would be accurate in saying that the person with this "tonality" in his or her triangle would be likely to show talent in dancing, singing, pottery, fashion design, cosmetology—creative movement of the body or some kind of creative self-expression that involves physical release, exercise, travel, photography, journalism, physical therapy through movement, etc. In another way a person with four 8s (8:4) would most likely indicate a good managerial, take-charge ability, interest in finance and investments (8) along with the capacity to roll up one's sleeves and do some of the physical hard work oneself (4). If the quantity of a certain energy is identical with the actual number (three 3s, or five 5s, for example), that energy is squared and greatly intensified. See figure 4.

Remember, in observing your "tonality keyboard," the number 0, which indicates that a certain numerical energy does not appear in your birth triangle, indicates a recessive

---

[3]The concept of "tonalities," comes from the spirit of Pythagorean teachings; they are proportions of how one energy is relating to another. This information was originally shared with me by the Reverend Flower A. Newhouse, founder of the Christward Ministry, Escondido, California. Reverend Newhouse encouraged me to work with the concepts of Pythagorean mathematics, and after almost twenty years, this presentation is at present the most clear description that I can offer as a tool for the reader's use and understanding.

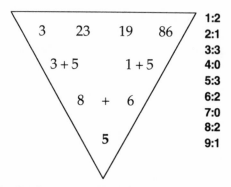

Figure 4. The Pythagorean triangle of a person born March 23, 1986 and the tonality keyboard.

energy, not a missing or deficient energy. This energy is present in you and in your life. Sometimes, this energy may have been thoroughly developed in your previous life experiences. However, this energy may also indicate areas that are more difficult for you. Look at this energy carefully and through study, reflection, and interactions with others, bring it forward into your life so that it is available when you need it.

Generally, in this book 10 is interpreted as a higher expression of 1, and is included as a 1 energy. (So to determine the quantity of 10s in your triangle, count the 1s.) The number 10, while not often mentioned in the text, is a latent energy that describes a larger capacity or potential for a person's life expression. It is helpful to compare the tonalities of 9 and 10 in your triangle. Observe the tonalities of 9 and 10 which express the relationship of your idealization (9) to your basic inborn capacity (10). Thus, two 10s (10:2) and two 9s (9:2) would most often indicate a likelihood that the desires and reach of the individual are compatible with the person's life capacity. The person's reach (9) corresponds with the basic, overall potentials for containment (10). One 10 (10:1) and three 9s (9:3) would indicate a deep desire to do more than is basically intended, or perhaps possible, while three 10s (10:3) and one 9 (9:1) might describe a situation where more is possible than the person may imagine or may be aspiring toward.

Tonalities of 1

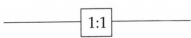

Your mind is very quick and catalytic. New ideas come into your consciousness like bright flashes of light—sudden, laser-like insights. Take down these promptings before they leave your mind.

Your creative thinking is very detailed. You may be sensitive about how others respond to your new ideas. Your thinking may be influenced by how your most significant partner feels, or by your needs for safety and security. You tend to move cautiously in your thinking.

Your verbal insights and ideas come to you in very creative, artistic forms. You most likely have speaking ability, and you can bring colorful words and imagery into your communication. You may speak to audiences or give talks and presentations in which you interact with others dramatically. You may write, journalize, or use pictures and poetic feelings to convey your ideas.

Original thinking combines with practical application of your thoughts to your work and tasks. You can make your ideas work in very useful ways. You can anchor and organize your original thoughts to create productive outcomes.

Your thinking and ideas contact a wide variety of people and situations. Sometimes your ideas may influence the promotional world of sales, foreign exchange, diversity in languages, cultures, and the media. You meet many different types of people and situations, and your versatile mind can handle them. Mentally, you adapt to change quickly. Your thoughts often have a varied, random quality to them. You are flexible, quick, and resourceful. You may have very good body-mind coordination, which at times can reveal athletic abilities.

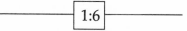

Your original thinking and pioneering ideas can be useful to families and groups. You are a catalytic counselor, communicator and teacher. You can also relate your thinking to social conditions, and your peers and contacts in the community may find you highly entertaining and stimulating. Your active mind can nurture and help others. Many of your ideas relate to family, home, and society.

A specialized, abstract and analytical thinking mode is one of your strongest abilities. You research new areas thoroughly, and you can gather new knowledge and present it in very original ways. You are a keen observer of life, and you use original concepts to convey wisdom. Like a laser, your mind penetrates through what it is viewing.

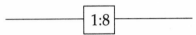

Your mental energy is quite dominant and authoritative. Your will is strong, and you may be controlling. Remember to honor others' ideas. Use the power of your mind to bless and empower, not to intimidate. You have many ideas and strong notions about business, investments and finances. Your ideas connect with businesses and the corporate world.

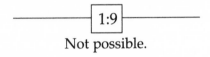

Not possible.

Tonalities of 2

You share verbally. You have an original approach toward details and data. Your innovative thinking and your independent stance need to harmonize with the needs and sensibilities of others. You waste no time in assessing and determining your very selective position. You may need to express your feelings of intimacy verbally—by talking and sharing your ideas with the person who is closest to you.

You are very sensitive and particular about comments, details, facts and any relationship that is important to you.

You may tend to take others' responses very personally and worry much over little matters. You may need to take life a bit less seriously. You are usually very sensitive and careful in areas that are important to you. You don't miss anything. Something has to be done just right—precisely the way you want it. You feel another's feelings very deeply. You are subjective and selective. You can anticipate another person's needs. You hurt when you hear about another's pain. Go slowly: Take one thing at a time. Avoid panic and fear by allowing spaces and taking opportunities to rest.

You can handle details and information in very creative and artistic ways. You can be both romantic and particular in your relationships. You can take ordinary moments and turn them into beautiful, expressive cameos that anyone would treasure. You are especially imaginative as a peacemaker and a harmonizer. You translate and interpret well. Intricacy and beauty combine; you feel the varied nuances of life very keenly. Your artistic side is often precise and is delicately expressed. You are very receptive to artistic tendencies, especially when you are with someone you can trust.

You are an excellent and purposeful organizer, especially in matters of detail and data-gathering. You can find use for many of the little pieces of life; you know how to fit and glue together many disparate elements and ingredients of the picture. People can depend on you to handle efficiently the nitty-gritty hassles, which require perseverance, precision, and sensitivity. You will work even harder for a person that is important to you. You feel more secure when your life is structured, planned, and predictable.

You have the ability to be flexible in the "sticky" areas of life. You can flow well with many people with different backgrounds and needs. Your good sense of humor can break up tight and worrisome moments. In the midst of little glitches, your versatility can help it all to happen. Maintain some freedom and movement in the midst of having to be careful and cautious. Exercise relieves bodily tension and emotional concerns. Adaptability helps you to be patient. Be sensitive to rhythm; flow in the moment, watching closely for particulars. Sex and affection are often related. You may like physical contact that is warm and steady, yet varied and exciting.

You are very particular and devoted to family and home. You will go to the end to please your friends and those who need you. When you work with groups, you can get to know each individual personally, instead of relating to a "herd." Your friends trust you deeply. Others can count on your loyalty, devotion, and performance. You may nurture the one you love with frequent parties and entertainment, especially in the home.

You may tend to be a perfectionist about details. You are also very private in your relationships. Your approach to communication may be quite introverted. Your depth of investigation matches your intention for perfection.

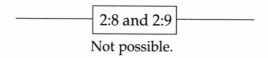

2:8 and 2:9

Not possible.

Tonalities of 3

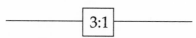

3:1

Creatively, your verbal and linguistic skills are evident. You are likely to have a way with words; you can express yourself creatively and artistically in highly articulate forms. Your innovative mind can color your language, and it influences people with a dramatic, convincing style. Writing and speaking may be two of your greatest abilities. Keep a life journal filled with words and pictures.

3:2

Creatively, you may be quite precise and detailed. You bring a selective sensitivity to your artistic expression, and you may be especially effective in creating cameos and vignettes of life. In your imagination you reveal precision and appropriateness. You combine good taste with artistic feelings. A personal, fulfilling partnership stimulates your creative drive and romance.

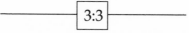

3:3

You are highly imaginative and creative, and your inner world of dreams and beauty is especially rich and varied. It may be easy for you to live in your own fantasies. Whatever you create is richly colored, dramatic, and filled with wonder. Create beauty in whatever you do. Express life's music and poetry. Your highly creative nature often can reveal scenes of wonder and enchantment. Find continuous expression for your artistic nature.

Your approach to creativity is quite organized and structured. You are imaginative in your tasks and projects. Your talents must find useful outlets, and you can influence activities by bringing into them color and visual power. Although a part of you might be unstructured and spontaneous, you also know how to be dependable and well-grounded. You accomplish your dreams purposefully. Your artistry expresses itself in orderly, productive ways.

Your creativity is versatile and active physically, and you express your imagination in a variety of ways. You contact many varied environments and backgrounds, seeing the colors of many walks of life. It is likely that you use your body in your creative efforts; you may travel, move around frequently, or be a representative for different interests and businesses. Some of your creativity may involve promotional activities. You relate creatively through personal contacts, variety, and exercise. You may enjoy enhancing the environment and beautifying the body.

You are especially creative with groups. You can inspire others with your artistic talents and entertainment. You also have creative gifts in teaching. You can use the arts to help society, especially your friends in the community.

Others are stirred by your creativity. Your dramatic sense may often come out in the company of an audience.

You can combine arts and psychology, science, and spirituality. Different dimensions of the creative arts yield insights into research and self-understanding. You can find depth and meaning in the ways you express your imaginative, artistic gifts. Your inner life and dreams are enriched by the creative arts.

Your creative gifts link with the business world and areas of authority. Part of you is very soft, and part of you is quite dominant.

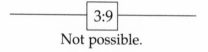

Not possible.

Tonalities of 4

You bring very innovative ideas to your work. You approach a job in new and exciting ways that make an ordinary task much more engaging and interesting. You like work that is challenging and new. You organize your projects in ways that are original and forward looking. You do not like to "re-invent the wheel." In your work, you thrive on independence and autonomy.

You are very detailed in your work. You want to do the job right, and you are sensitive about your performance. You make sure to get all the details in order as you approach a task. You also have a good sense of the capabilities of others. You pick a reliable partner, and are sympathetic to the particular needs involved in doing the task well. You are a caring, sensitive provider.

You approach a task very creatively with much imagination. You do your work colorfully, with joy, especially if you like it. You can inspire others to release their creative talents as the work gets done. You combine structure with free-flow imagination and feeling. You can be purposeful, yet romantic and happy.

Your life may largely be taken up with your work. You may spend long hours on projects and tasks. It may be difficult for you to know what to do when you are not involved in your work. Develop some pleasurable hobbies that are not related to the project. Learn how to play more and avoid tendencies toward living like a robot. Be more flexible. Do not allow duty to the job to freeze your feelings. You can be loved for yourself—not just for what you do.

You can mix your schedules and routines with play and spontaneity. You get the job done in a variety of ways, and you may do ordinary routine work in different settings with different people. Changes may come suddenly at times, requiring you to adjust quickly, in order to finish the project. Work and physical movement may be related. Demands may confront you from many sides. Maintain a sense of humor. Take time to exercise.

You work well with groups of people. Your social skills are many and varied, and you know how to be a friend to others while getting the job done. Your friends will work hard for you, and they trust you to be loyal and fair. With your family and in your friendships you are steadfast and trustworthy.

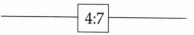

You work with a sense of perfection. You bring a deep understanding to what you do, combining outward labor with inner knowledge and wisdom. You may be highly mechanical. You are intuitive and sometimes more abstract, yet you are very practical and down-to-earth. Remember to bring out your feelings and have some fun.

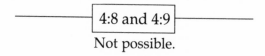

Not possible.

Tonalities of 5

You balance a body/mind approach to life. Physical release is connected to mental stimulation. You are quick and at times restless; you need to keep your mind and body frequently activated. You enjoy a challenge, and are always alert and ready to move. In sports, for example, you can play a thinking game, as well as a very physical one. You ask many questions of many people. You can capture the contemporary scene in colorful words and concepts. You like to keep current, and you welcome new ideas from a variety of contacts. You think and move very quickly.

You approach contact and change somewhat carefully. Part of you may be more like a free spirit, craving sensation, while another side of you, sensitive and emotional, may be more cautious, even skeptical. You may spend much time trying to keep many areas of life in order, one by one; you notice many pieces, and you are often trying to gather and fit them together in a way that gives you a sense of security. You are inclined to be more physical when you trust and feel close to someone special.

You use many creative approaches to meet the public. Imagination helps you adapt to changing conditions. Your artistic abilities are stimulated by variety, travel, and physical movement. You bring together beauty and the playful dance of life. Physicality combines with romance and wonder. You express beauty in movement. Working creatively with your body may open doors in the healing arts, health care, sports, or the world of fashion and design. Find creative release through your body. Celebrate your life.

You may spend much time organizing confusion and rapidly changing circumstances. Your contacts with many people can be used practically. Your many interests are productive, and you are dependable, even while wearing many hats. You "get it done," although at times people may have difficulty pinning you down or labeling you.

You may seem to be in perpetual motion. You are on the go much of the time, highly charged, and in need of releasing much nervous energy through your body. You may also be easily excitable, often stirring up the atmosphere around you. Exercise, on a regular basis, helps remove your sense of panic and frustration. You do not enjoy limitations. Keep many doors and interests open. Get out of the house. Enjoy the out of doors and nature. An earthy sense of humor relieves irritability and temper. You yourself may create many of the changes to which you must respond. Satisfy your appetites appropriately. Avoid gambling, spending sprees, and other addictive tendencies that satisfy your craving for newness and sensation. Calm and easy solutions may bore you.

You may be involved in many activities with groups or with family. Movement, adventure, travel, etc., combine with group and community involvement. Part of you might prefer to be free, while another side of you wants friends and likes to be accepted by others.

A restless, kinetic side of you is balanced by an investigative, reflective nature. You move around, but you also know how to still yourself and rest.

Not possible.

Tonalities of 6

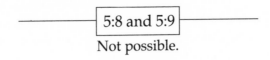

You relate well with people through your creative, innovative thinking. You are a natural teacher, counselor, and entertainer who stimulates friends, groups, and the larger community with your mind. You are a natural catalyst with others. You especially enjoy people who interest you. Your original ideas can motivate others. You like groups that move and think on the "cutting edges."

You can be sensitive to one particular individual as well as comfortable with groups and friends. You will take pains for others and you try to help them whenever possible. You have precise information that can relate closely to the needs around you. You have the facts, and you can communicate them clearly to people. You may be too easily influenced by how the family, peers, or the group feels.

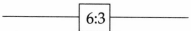

You are very creative and dramatic with groups. You know how to inspire people and help them to release their talents. You can use your artistic abilities to help society. Your dreams for others and your vision make many possibilities come alive. You may be especially effective as an artist-guide who introduces others to what is beautiful and culturally meaningful.

Your ability to organize and plan ahead helps different family members and groups achieve their goals. A realistic sense of what is workable and useful helps you motivate and direct others. You are a worker in the family and community. Many depend on you. You are reliable, and you care.

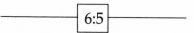

You bring a sense of playfulness and fun into many different groups of people. You are especially good at coordinating the varied activities of the group. You can follow socially acceptable norms, but you also are a free spirit who likes to do your own thing. You have many friends, but sometimes they may not know exactly what to expect from you. Communicate your needs and feelings to others.

You are very much involved with family, friends, and groups in the community. You can work for social causes, and you may find yourself nurturing others much of your lifetime. Take some time for you. Free yourself from too many responsibilities and invasions of your space.

You can mix social contacts with your deep thirst for knowledge and privacy. You can research groups effectively.

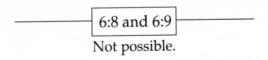

Not possible.

Tonalities of 7

Your original thinking connects with research and scientific study into fields of specialized knowledge. There is a somewhat abstract side to your personality—a private, interior world that is going on inside you as you also function in the outer world. Bring out feelings, not just analytical, interior responses. Your approach to spirituality may be quite daring and original. You forge your own path.

You are very detailed in your knowledge. You may be cautious about taking a stand or revealing your innermost thoughts. You are quite particular and sensitive when sharing your deepest feelings. You may come across as quite removed and introverted. Remember to communicate with others.

Arts, psychology, and spirituality combine in your consciousness to reveal mysteries through creative expression.

Many of your feelings and artistic talents open doors into deeper truth. You have the ability to describe artistically some of the deeper metaphysical dimensions of life. Your imagination often connects with the inner world. Your intuition may contact deeper, unconscious, layers of feeling. You may choose to use mandalas, or drawings and paintings, to suggest a larger vision of wholeness.

You bring to your work a sense of perfection. You apply your mechanical knowledge with precision. You may be quite methodical and silent, doing the job in solitude to accomplish the deeper, lasting outcome. You approach psychological and spiritual needs with planning and useful activity. At times, as you work, you may feel that you are in another world.

You can take your deep knowledge and diversify it into many fields and directions of activity. You can communicate your knowledge to a variety of people and conditions. You may be very playful, yet also quite serious and quiet. Science and health may provide interesting connections.

Your contacts with family and groups offer you opportunities to share your knowledge. A certain private side in you combines with a warmer, more friendly side. You can be comfortable in the company of others, and you enjoy quiet times alone, in your own space.

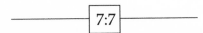

You have a very penetrating mind that searches deeply into specialized areas.

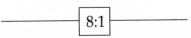

Not possible.

Tonalities of 8

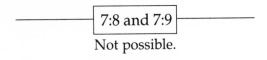

Your original ideas can be an entrepreneurial asset to businesses and the corporate structure. You are a good troubleshooter. You set others in motion with your creative possibilities. You are independent and authoritative in part, and you have much to offer those who are receptive. Remember to work cooperatively with people, even if they do not always accept your futuristic thinking. You are a creative investor. Learn to use money wisely.

You are most likely cautious and careful about asserting your power and position. You are sensitive to another person's feelings, especially when you have to assert yourself in someone's presence. Having a close partner that you trust helps you step forward. You demand precision and care for details. Know when to defer and when to set boundaries. Take your stand.

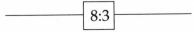

Part of you is quite dominant, while another part of you may seem to be more elusive and free-floating. You can, therefore, be soft or hard, easy going or authoritative, romantic or controlling, depending upon how you integrate these very different sides of yourself. Let others know where you are coming from. Be clear about feelings and expectations. Temper your need for power with an ability to be more adaptable and unstructured.

You can use power and position in very dependable, purposeful ways. Your rules are solid and well-defined, and you stick by them. You state clear boundaries and set firm policies. What you work at, you execute and complete. You may be demanding, but you are also dedicated and thorough. You labor long for successful outcomes.

You know how to mean business, but you also know how to play. When your power is threatened, you can use humor and flexibility to avoid irritation and outbursts. Your authority may be tested by a wide variety of people, and some of your jurisdiction may require traveling and handling sudden changes. You coordinate discipline of body, mind, and will-power. When your position is threatened, avoid eruptive, abusive behaviors.

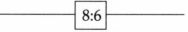

You wield your power and authority with family, relatives, and groups. You are firm, but kind and friendly. Sometimes it may bother you to make a decision that doesn't please others. You want to be helpful. You may encounter circumstances where you must be the manager who takes control. When possible, make decisions from group consensus.

You have a very specialized expertise in certain fields of business. Your knowledge helps you to administer authority and position.

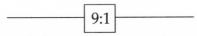

Not possible.

Tonalities of 9

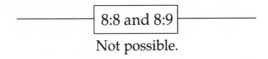

You have original ideas and concepts that can help humanity. You help others in need, but sometimes on your own terms, in your own ways. Certain areas of your life come to an end suddenly, and then new doors open. You may be a catalyst for those who have lost hope. With your words, you can enflame others' minds with new inspiration.

Your perspective is broad, yet you also pay close attention to personal details. You enjoy close partnership with another person, yet you also spend part of your life reaching out in a much larger arena of activity. You may combine close, intimate caring with impartial, even detached, response. You may have to balance your time with the needs of the many and those closest to you.

You can benefit humanity with your creative, artistic gifts. Your imagination is very fertile, especially when you apply it to areas of service and others' needs. You are inspired as you are exposed to the needs and behaviors of others. Your use of the arts can inspire and uplift others.

You are a hard worker, especially for the needs of humanitarian causes. Your reliable sense of planning and scheduling ensures productive outcomes, particularly in difficult areas of service. You are especially purposeful and effective in addressing the needs of others. Sometimes your hard work may not yield predictable outcomes.

In the midst of many interruptions and unexpected changes, you apply yourself and your energies in service. You may meet a wide variety of people who may require you to be flexible. You may travel to other places, experiencing a variety of cultural patterns. Life keeps you alert and adaptable. Rarely are circumstances or outcomes predictable.

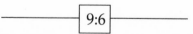

You work with family, groups, and humanity in general. Your kindness and caring extend to many different lives and many different needs. Your humanitarian efforts find expression with people that you know well, and you work with many strangers.

Your work with humanity includes some very specialized areas of knowledge. You have a private side that most people know nothing about. Your mind penetrates many difficulties that require unique solutions.

In working with many different people, you must sometimes define your boundaries and your limits. Many people make demands on your time and energy. Keep your policies clear.

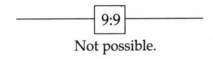

Not possible.

CYCLES

Additional important information that can be gleaned from your birthdate comes from the four cycles of life opportunity. Timing is very important to your journey. During certain years of your life, a particular numerical tone is stronger, providing you with a specific focus and special areas of opportunity and challenge.

All human beings go through common stages of life, or "rites of passage." Developmentally, these include such experiences as birth, infancy, preschool, elementary school, adolescence, young adulthood, mid-life, old age, and transition into the inner worlds. Each of us can point to significant moments within these stages, such as early bonding and assertiveness, gaining skills, passing through rites of puberty, falling in love, leaving home, getting a first job and paycheck, graduating from school, marrying, becoming a parent, perhaps going through a divorce, losing a loved one, experiencing an illness, moving to a new location, etc. We can observe four mystical stages in a person's life: the dream; leaving the dream (exile); experiencing crisis; and healing and transformation.

Underlying all these universal changes, like circles moving within circles, an individual's own particular rhythms and cycles are also present. These timings are unique to each person's own life path and offer new possibilities for greater progress.

In the spirit of Pythagorean numerics, each individual moves through at least four major cycles. Each cycle identifies periods of focused opportunity in key areas, during specific years of the lifetime. The more we can identify and keep in mind such cycles, the more we can be alert and better prepared for what may be coming to us. Obviously, we cannot know everything ahead, but by sensing some of the thematic material that is there in our life pattern, we might avoid being blindsided. We can perhaps take preparatory steps that will be beneficial for facing the times ahead. Therefore, every person is wise to try and sense the tone and scope of the years ahead, as well as evaluate the years that are here now and to learn from what has already come and gone. Try to get some perspective of the tapestry of your life; feel the natural flow and progressions of your cycles. Respond as openly and deeply as possible; try to see the lessons and the perspective. What is your life experience trying to teach you? Watch most closely for the most critical times when one cycle is ending and a new one is beginning. In these times, energies are shifting, sometimes drastically, and your life may be full of sudden changes. Using the principles of Pythagorean numerics, try to sense where the energies of your life best need to move.

Life Cycles

Here is a simple way to find the **years** and the **tone** of each of your four major cycles. In order to help illustrate each of the four steps I will refer you to the fictional person whose birthdate is March 23, 1986.

Cycle I: Subtract the number of your **Birth Force** (the number at the bottom of your triangle) from 36. (Example: 36 − 5 = 31). Incidentally, "36" is derived from a base of four cycles, nine years each $(9 + 9 + 9 + 9 = 36)$. However, the **duration** of the first cycle extends from birth (0) to the particular age derived from subtracting the person's Birth Force from 36. This will be different for each Birth Force, 1–9. Thus, the number of years of the first cycle will always be longer than the following three cycles, each of which lasts for nine years. For example, the first cycle for a person with a Birth Force of 5 would be 0–31 years (36 − 5 = 31). (see Table 1 for the duration of Cycle I corresponding with each Birth Force).

To find the tone of Cycle I, add the month and day of your birthdate. Find the total reduced to a single digit. For example, the birthdate of March 23, 1986 would have a tone of 8 for Cycle I (see figure 5 on page 54).

The **tone** of **Cycle I** is *critically important*, especially for children, parents, teachers, and counselors (see table 2 on p. 55). The **tone** of the first cycle identifies clearly various needs and predispositions that are crucially important for understanding the uniqueness and individuality of each child. By knowing the tone of the first cycle, any caretaker is better able to provide for a child's needs. Often, with this knowledge, a child will feel more confident and receptive to suggestions that are beneficial to his or her life journey.

Table 1. Duration of the First Cycle.

Birth Force Number	Duration of the First Cycle (in years)*
1	0–35
2	0–34
3	0–33
4	0–32
5	0–31
6	0–30
7	0–29
8	0–28
9	0–27

*The duration of the first cycle is derived by subtracting the Birth Force number from 36.

Summary	Cycle	Years		Tone
	I	0–31	=	8

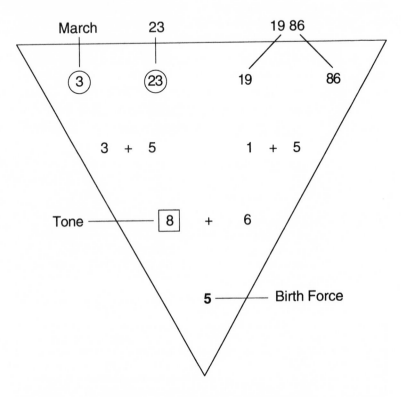

Figure 5. The tone and duration of a person's first cycle whose birthdate is March 23, 1986. The month (3) and day (23) breaks down to (3 + 5) which equals 8—the tone of Cycle I.

Table 2. First Cycle Roles Children May Play.*

Energy	CONSTRUCTIVE	DENIED OR THWARTED
1	**Student:** quick mind, eager to learn; must be challenged mentally; thrives on new ideas; thinks for oneself; entrepreneurial; must gain independence through own thinking.	**Troublemaker:** "smart mouth" who argues and talks back; easily bored, impatient, impulsive; sees through sham and stupidity, but comes across as brash or very argumentative; cannot tolerate others' shortcomings; tunnel vision; "ornery" and overly autonomous.
2	**Trusted Partner:** needs one close friend; must be the helper who is needed; looks to one person for deep bonding. **Affiliator:** links emotionally by doing and feeling close to someone else; listens closely and feels the troubles of another; sympathetic and must be in touch. **Critical Thinker:** sees the small details and clearly senses the situation; highly selective; gets the facts, arranges and categorizes information; compartmentalizes the parts. **Sensitive Receptor:** highly receptive artistically; "picks up" on feelings, moods and nuances in a situation or atmosphere.	**Baby:** wants too much attention; spoiled by too much pampering; needy and often sickly to get attention; emotionally dependent on another. **Victim:** absorbs another's pain/anger by receiving abuse and mistreatment; allows others to take advantage and "dump" on him/her; displays masochistic tendencies; equates love with abuse; needs to be hurt. **Scapegoat:** speaks clearly and gets the blame; receives punishment for being blunt and critical; may become hypercritical and obsessive; may worry too much; opinionated. **Phobic:** fears persons and situations; carries an imminent sense of dread; tends to see only the dark side of life; frequently doubts; "Eeyore" syndrome: sees only the "down side" of life.

*For additional descriptions of behaviors and roles associated with the different energies see my book *Living Your Destiny*, also published by Samuel Weiser.

Table 2. First Cycle Roles Children May Play (continued).

Energy	CONSTRUCTIVE	DENIED OR THWARTED
3	**Creative Artist:** highly creative and imaginative; very dramatic; artistically expressive. **Dreamer:** can easily live in an inner world of beauty; resides in nature, poetry, music, romantic feelings, etc.; emphasizes the imagination.	**Histrionic:** prima donna, who demands limelight all the time; exaggerates the scene; may become emotionally "strung out." **Fantasizer:** may "space out" to avoid reality; uses the mood-altering state to avoid unpleasant responsibilities; may be more in love with love than with an actual person; may become delusional.
4	**Organizer:** capable doer who "gets it together;" workhorse, who always completes the task; always busy doing something constructive; expects structure and dependability from others. **Achiever:** seeks accomplishment; completes everything well; goal-oriented and purposeful; keeps many projects going until they are finished.	**Robot:** more like a machine; buries frozen feelings; can't stop from activities, duties, and tasks. **Super-Achiever:** never can do enough; equates worthiness with busyness; workaholic; takes no breaks; never has any fun; humorless; makes life a drudgery; everything is an effort; allows no free time for play or leisure.
5	**Innovator:** finds new options and solutions in the moment; unconventional yet effective; quick and resourceful; communicates with many kinds of people and situations; likes speed and adventure. **Humorist:** relieves tensions and diffuses heaviness through fun and humor; offers comedy (often earthy)	**Rebel/Maverick:** too eccentric; bumps against status quo; brash and offensive; confrontive; must be different; stirs up and disrupts the atmosphere; creates chaos and confusion; starts too many options at once. **Clown:** acts out craziness in self and others; expresses anger physically and verbally through wild behaviors; may

Table 2. First Cycle Roles Children May Play (continued).

Energy	CONSTRUCTIVE	DENIED OR THWARTED
5 (cont)	and playfulness; can mimic and imitate sounds and people; stand-up comic. **Taster:** wants the physical, sensory experience; feels life through the viscera of the body and through movement; keeps many irons in the fire and has many interests going at once; must experience physical appetites: eating, tasting, smelling, touching, hearing. **Exerciser/Athlete/Sports Enthusiast:** restless and kinetic; body must move to keep healthy; person develops physical skills and prowess; bodily drives find healthy outlets in experiencing nutritional food, sensible exercise, healthful hygiene and rest; person thrives on massage and physical therapy; person enjoys spas, jacuzzis, etc. **Humorist/Comic:** sees fun, playfulness, and humor as essential in life.	receive abuse by attracting others' anger and violent tendencies; caustic responses arouse others' tempers. **Addict:** excessive and out of bounds with appetites; "blows out" and then collapses in exhaustion; wastes time, money and energy in feeding the appetites; life is scattered and unfocused; many breakups occur in relationships; person spreads out too much in all directions; debts remain unpaid in the midst of free spending; drugs/alcohol/pills. **Jock:** the crowd pleaser; "super-athlete" who is "hulk" and "stud"; craves repeated sex and feeds off the bodies and exploitation of others; abuses those who are vulnerable, lonely, or naive; seeks cheap thrills at the expense of others; out of control; treats persons as amusements, then "trashes" whomever/whatever becomes boring or needful; likes fights; treats opposite sex (or same sex) abusively; can be bisexual.
6	**Caregiver:** takes care of those who are helpless or neglected; a true friend to those in need; affectionate and nurturing; has good self-esteem; a naturally kind person who cares.	**Pleaser:** gets approval by placating and saying what others want to hear; "surrogate" who takes over others' responsibilities; relieves others' problems.

Table 2. First Cycle Roles Children May Play (continued).

Energy	CONSTRUCTIVE	DENIED OR THWARTED
6 (cont)	**Social Server:** serves needs of family, group and society. **Host/Hostess:** entertains others in the home, providing fellowship, good conversation, and pleasing company. **Loyal Family Member:** included by others and inclusive; sees others as potential friends, and sees the world as friendly.	**Narcissist:** draws attention to oneself; must be recognized and acknowledged; cannot address needs of others. **Sociopath:** uses society and family to meet own needs; sees people as a means to get ahead; may be very antisocial, unable or unwilling to be loyal to persons, family or groups. **Status Seeker:** resents the success of others, yet uses them to get ahead; toadies to those in authority; undermines those with reputation. **Slob:** social misfit, unable to take part in conversation and exhibiting lack of manners, poor social graces, and messy, uncouth behaviors, usually done in protest against status quo. **Enmeshed/Shamed Member:** held in the prison of the family and home; shamed by the family.
7	**Student/Scholar:** from the beginning, needs much time and space alone; happy in own company. **Bringer of Wisdom and Knowledge:** usually knows what is "right" and expresses divine order.	**Invisible Child:** not noticed and left to his/her own devices; not spoken to or included in the family routines; feels alienated and abandoned and goes exclusively into own world of study or spirituality; creates own world to live in.

Table 2. First Cycle Roles Children May Play (continued).

Energy	CONSTRUCTIVE	DENIED OR THWARTED
8	**Manager:** must be in charge and make decision early; is often accurate and strong in values and policies; needs own areas of power in family; needs to make money; does well with own savings account; may early begin own business or will find own ways to make money; responds well to being given options and making choices; enjoys winning, but empowers others; interested in law and justice, perhaps politics.	**Defiant Child:** often angry and disgusted with the family; feels essentially smarter than parents and will not obey; must run the household; family often intimidated and does not follow through with discipline, boundaries or policies earlier established; child often seeks revenge on those who try to keep him/her in line; child manipulates parents, especially if they are divided between each other; win-lose interactions; must always win at the expense of someone else.
9	**Rescuer:** feels for the underdog and tries to save others from pain and suffering; will give unselfishly for the totality, not just for own personal gains; extremely empathic; enjoys serving and meeting others' needs.	**Meddler:** robs others of their lessons in the name of "helpfulness"; merges with the need and thus loses own center and focus of identity. **Martyr:** takes the pain and abuse of others in the name of service; may forfeit own power, health, money, etc.; life may be "put on hold" in early years, as others may abandon him/her or cast him/her aside; may have to spend much time caring for sick family members or own sickness.

Cycle II: Cycle II lasts for nine years. Continuing with our example of a person born March 23, 1986, **Cycle II** would occur between the ages of 32–41.

Summary	Cycle	Years		Tone
	I	0–31	=	**8**
	II	32–41	=	**2**

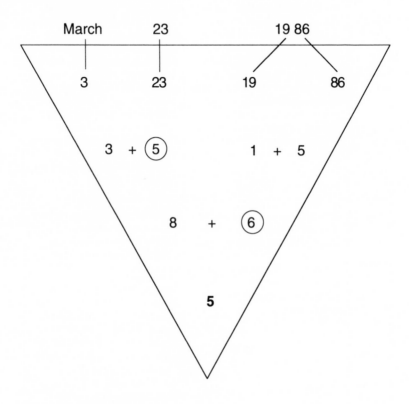

Figure 6. The tone and duration of a person's second cycle whose birthdate is March 23, 1986. The day reduces to the single digit 5 and the year to 6. When added together, 5 + 6 = 11 which in turn reduces to 2 (1 + 1 = 2)—the tone of Cycle II.

Summary	Cycle	Years		Tone
	I	0–31	=	8
	II	32–41	=	2
	III	42–51	=	10 = 1
	IV	52–61	=	9

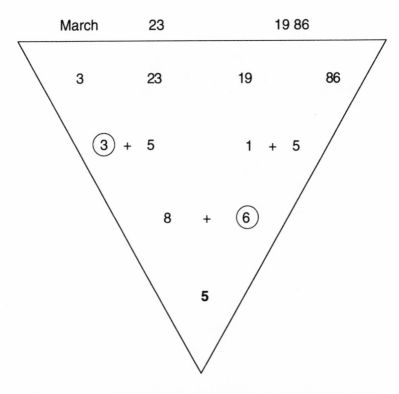

March   23   19 86

Figure 7. The tone and duration of a person's fourth cycle whose birthdate is March 23, 1986. The month is 3 and the year reduces to the single digit 6. When added together, the new figure is 9—the tone of the Cycle IV.

Cycle I: 0–31
Cycle II: 32–41 (32 + 9 = 41)

To find the **tone** of **Cycle II**, <u>add the day (5) and the year (6)</u> (5 + 6 = 11 = **2**). See figure 6 on p. 60.

Cycle III: Cycle III also lasts for nine years. Continuing our example, here are the years for **Cycle III:**

Cycle I: 0–31
Cycle II: 32–41
Cycle III: 42–51 (42 + 9 = 51)

To find the **tone** of **Cycle III**, add together the tones of **Cycle I** and **Cycle II**. Again, if the total is 10 or greater, reduce the number to a single digit.

Summary	Cycle	Years		**Tone**
	I	0–31	=	**8**
	II	32–41	=	**2**
	III	42–51	=	**10 = 1**

Cycle IV: Cycle IV lasts for nine years.

Cycle I: 0–31
Cycle II: 32–41
Cycle III: 42–51
Cycle IV: 52–61 (52 + 9 = 61)

To find the **tone** of **Cycle IV**, add together the numbers of **Month** and **Year**. Find the total and reduce below 10 (3 + 1986 = 27 = **9**). See figure 7 on p. 61.

Interpreting the Cycles and Their Tones

The specific numerical tone of each cycle is like a keynote that sounds its particular themes of opportunity and challenge during the years that this tone is being activated. In general, the most challenging times in each person's life are those that occur during the transitional years, that is, the year or years when a person is ending one cycle and beginning the next one. Thus, in our illustration, the most challenging times would be the crossover years as indicated below:

8 ⟶	2 ⟶	1 ⟶	9 ⟶	Last Cycle completed
0– 31	○ 32– 41	○ 42– 51	○ 52– 61	○ 62- completion of lifetime.

During these transitional years a shift of energy takes place. Transitional times may require added flexibility in the midst of sudden changes. An individual who is more aware of the implications and thematic material of the cycles can be more perceptive; and in this spirit it is likely that everything "will come to pass" more quickly and more smoothly. The greater our awareness, the less likelihood there is of upheaval. It is especially helpful to try to integrate the content of the previous cycle with the content of the cycle that is coming in. New energies can be better received and harmonized with those patterns and formations already active in us. When the four cycles have passed, it is most common for a person to move ahead without any particular tone or cycle. All the nine energies are likely to be active in the person's life.

Tone 1 Cycles

A 1 tone emphasizes themes of autonomy and independent thinking. When the 1 tone appears in the Cycle I, these themes are even more stimulated in early childhood, particularly the toddler and pre-school years (approximately ages 18 months to 6 years old). A toddler who has a 1 tone in the Cycle I will begin early to explore and take initiative. Most likely such a child will have special verbal skills and will need to talk, argue, dispute, and play with words. Such a child, within reasonable boundaries, must not be stifled, discouraged, or shamed. The entrepreneurial need is strong, and such a child must be encouraged to take chances, risk, and make mistakes on the road to continuous learning. Such a young person will most likely be a quick and avid learner; thus, it is essential that parents and other providers provide constant mental and verbal stimulus. Simple keys to learning—reading out loud, imitating sounds, discussing ideas and various viewpoints, cultures and belief systems, learning other languages, reading, memorizing poetry, studying music and drama—are all extremely important. Make sure there are always new books, videos, and tapes around. Talk shows, quiz shows, and other educational programming will be most helpful. With a 1 tone, a person is always challenged by reaching ahead into the future. Mental boredom comes quickly if there is much repetition. Avoid lecturing to 1 tone people—discuss! Challenge their thinking! Debate! A young person with a 1 tone usually will think for him or herself, and it would be difficult to try to change his or her thinking. The thought processes are rapid; they are often more randomly and spontaneously intuitive than logical and sequential.

In later cycles a 1 tone often indicates the need to realize independence, which may mean trying a new area of employment or making a move in a new direction, location, or field of learning. In my own experience, I have found that the 1 tone in any cycle will offer many opportunities for new directions of autonomy in thinking, education, and pioneering mental enterprise. The doors of Providence open often unexpectedly, but an individual must be alert, daring, and quick to actualize the potential. Thinking that remains provincial, rigid or circumscribed impedes many opportunities from happening. Risk is essential; overcome tentativeness and be willing to move forward to new horizons. Any 1 tone calls for the individual to take initiative and seize the opportunity presented.

------------------------ Tone 2 Cycles ------------------------

Any 2 tone emphasizes themes of intimacy, emotional closeness and security, trust, supportiveness, partnership, patience, and detailed information. If a 2 tone appears in Cycle I in the infancy stage of development (0–2 years), the child is especially needy. The desire for an immediate bonding with a safe, trustworthy, comforting caretaker is extreme. If deep, emotional connection with someone does not occur quickly, any infant will feel alarm and panic. But when the 2 tone occurs as Cycle I, and such bonding needs are not met or are delayed too long, fears of abandonment are likely to haunt the child for many years. Later, even in adulthood, intimacy may be difficult for such a person, who may still be extremely needy and emotionally wary. A nagging watchfulness is likely to eat at this person who worries in every relationship, "Will this person be there for me?" or "Will this person leave me?" or "What more can I do, so that the person will need me?" or "Will I be rejected, abandoned, and left all alone?" Such are the frequent worries, even panic attacks, that may accompany an individual whose first cycle carries the unfulfilled 2 tone.

When a significant caretaker is present early, and close bonding occurs, it may then be difficult for the affiliative person with 2 tone ever to bond with anyone else. It is the basic nature of a person who is strong in the energy of TWOness to look for ONE other close partner. The ONE, trustworthy "other" often becomes everything for the affiliator. In this way a very strong mother figure (or sometimes a father figure) may bond so closely with a child that the young one is consumed by the other, thus failing to develop a sufficiently strong ego and identity. Thus, in the case of an especially needy child, a loving caregiver must provide warmth and closeness without taking over the life. While offering love and sympathy, such a caregiver must also build confidence in the child and know when *not* to be present or stiflingly intrusive. It is a real challenge in any relationship to balance closeness with distance. We can converge with someone, but we must not merge with another. To be emotionally supportive does not mean to take over another's psychological and emotional space. If a needy child bonds too deeply with a parent figure, it may be very difficult for such a youngster to relinquish or "divorce" this person later, in order to bond deeply and appropriately with someone else in natural adult partnership with an equal. Often, even if the first emotional bonding is a negative or abusive one, a needy child may become the emotional "surrogate spouse" to an abusive or neglectful parent. Any later relationship for the child may be difficult, as it may seem to resemble an almost adulterous union and a betrayal of the original emotional commitment. Or, such a child may look for someone else who is equally negative or abusive. Love is then equated with mistreatment and needing to become a victim.

In any cycle that carries a 2 tone, it is essential to build one's own confidence through close partnership. By supporting the leader, a good partner gains and feels secure. If the basic energies are more independent, during a cycle carrying the 2 tone, a person is wise to yield and come close through a more attentive, cooperative attitude. The years of any 2 tone are times calling for patience, attentiveness, receptivity, sensitivity for the needs of the other, and the willingness to please and act unselfishly. Great gain can come from being appropriately helpful to others. Humility opens the doors to power and fulfillment.

Tone 3 Cycles

The 3 tone in any cycle highlights creativity and artistic self-expression. Creative opportunities provide outlets for imagination, dramatic power, romance, and the gala and pageantry of life. If the 3 tone comes as the first cycle, the child will almost always show an inclination for some form of the arts. Therefore, it is most important to observe these early, creative responses: Does your child show a special interest in music, theater, acting, clay or drawing, singing, dancing, etc.? Notice the response! **Feed the early interests**! I remember so clearly a little girl that I once counseled. She was not obeying her parents. They were well-meaning, but essentially joyless. The little girl was ultradramatic, even histrionic, in her responses which typically included elevated voice tone, sudden, turn-on tears, followed by high-pitched laughter—all the colorful behaviors that embarrassed and puzzled her quiet, serious, stolid parents. As I worked with her, I noticed a strong 3 energy vibration and a 3 tone first cycle. I suggested that she try out for a school play. At first, my suggestion seemed a total non sequitur to the charge of disobedience, but with a sneer, the parents tried the suggestion. Their daughter became an overnight success, playing the lead role of fairy princess in the school drama of the year. She received a standing ovation. She then began to obey much more naturally, especially when her parents found a new audition for her. Counseling sessions fizzled out, as there was no longer any major difficulty. The little girl's dramatic nature had found acceptance and could be channeled into appropriate outlets.

I believe in many cases the answer lies in finding the natural flow and direction for our energies. Frustrated or misdirected energies lead to frustrated persons. Find the creative attraction; identify your interests and find what really excites you. As much as possible, focus your energies into these channels of creative self-expression. Keep a balance between structure and playful nonstructure each day.

As the 3 tone occurs in later cycles of life, previous impressions and experiences will tend to find artistic expression. It is often to a person's advantage to experience a 3 tone cycle later in life, since there is usually more material to draw from life experience. Such a cycle usually is accompanied by feelings of wanting more time, open space, and less structure in daily life. The muse of inspiration thrives on receptivity and spontaneity; thus, keeping some space and time open invites the creative, poetic inspiration. Keep your life as clear as possible in the presence of any cycle that carries a 3 tone. Follow your dream and express your artistic abilities.

Tone 4 Cycles

The 4 tone in any cycle quickens achievement. It is a good time in a person's life to accomplish concrete results through work and structured activity. Any cycle that keynotes the 4 tone can be a demanding time of life. Dependability and long hours are frequently required. Yet if an individual can respond steadfastly and finish the task, he or she becomes a dynamic warrior of the Spirit, motivated by a strong sense of purpose. If the 4 tone comes as Cycle I, the child will benefit from a structured, directed, goal-oriented environment. Without becoming obsessive or "driving" parents, such adults can spur a child on to build a firm foundation that can achieve lasting results. Their child does not have to become a neurotic overachiever, never measuring up. But he or she will most likely want to improve skills and will enjoy seeing progressive, concrete results. Rewards and praise, a weekly allowance, stickers, stars, certificates, acknowledgment for making the honor roll, excelling in sports or hobbies, or winning a contest—all of these and more can provide proof of good effort. Bumper stickers proudly recognizing FOURness may read, "My child was an outstanding student at _____ school!" It is also important for parents to *love children for themselves*, not just for what they do. A major distortion of the 4 tone is to equate any person's worth with what they do, not who they are. Every person needs to feel love and acceptance for personhood—for the incredibly special human being that we are, beautiful the way God has made us, now—not for how we may be in the future, if we do enough or please someone else. Later in life a 4 tone usually means hard work, more structure, demands on one's time, deadlines to be met, etc., but it also indicates a time of great potential productivity, when efforts will be rewarded.

Tone 5 Cycles

In every cycle the 5 tone is filled with variety, movement, and tastes of new life experiences. When the 5 tone occurs as the Cycle I, times can be hectic. A child in 5 tone may personally be very kinetic and restless, needing much room and space. His or her body must discharge much energy, so sports, gymnastics, outdoor activities, and opportunities to explore must be provided. Caregivers must observe good health habits, so that the child will not "burn out" or risk damage to the body through dangerous, thrill-seeking, and excessive sexual sensations. Regular rest, good diet and sensible exercise stabilize such a child's basic restlessness, flurries of activity, and scattered living. A young child cannot always control bodily movements, and a very active, perpetually moving body can experience collisions and accidents. Sometimes, parents mistake large outbursts of nervous energy and bodily excesses for rebelliousness or failure to listen. Unnecessary abuse, such as slaps and spankings, only serve to excite this type of child even more. The need for freedom and an appetite for sensation make the child a "push-pull" experience for others as he or she seeks closeness and contact on the run. The youngster is usually not a cuddler or a sitter. Fun and thrills satisfy much more than long conversations and quiet company. It is helpful to diversify the energy—keep many irons hot so the child can rebound from one interest to another. When 5 tone is strong, people rarely complete much of what they start.

In adulthood a 5 tone often signifies change of location: a job change, travel, new acquaintances, position shifts, a need for more flexibility and increased physical movement. It may be a time when more energy is needed to sustain relationships and maintain the home and family. Avoid upheavals, panicky responses, and excessive cravings. Take things as they come, meet the needs of the moment, and move forward. Certain patterns may have to break up in order for new energies to come in. Take care of body and health.

Tone 6 Cycles

The 6 tone, in any cycle, emphasizes the family, friends, and groups. If this tone appears as the Cycle I, there is always a strong connection between the child and the home. The child is highly impressionable and often feels responsible for the well-being of others. Parents may either nurture the child or destructively enmesh the child through shaming, doting, expecting too much, confining the child inside family secrets or trapping the child within an addictive, highly dysfunctional environment. The basic needs for such a child, who begins with the 6 tone, are to have friends, a nurturing atmosphere, and opportunities to please and to build self-esteem. Too much conformity within the family structure is not healthy. The child also grows socially by becoming a helper, doing chores and adding to the well-being of the household and community. It is also very important for such a child to excel during the elementary school years. This is the time when every child benefits from learning skills and interacting with empowering peers, adults, mentors, and hero models, whom he or she can learn from and emulate. Kindness and genuine affection are immensely valuable to any child, especially at this age. Contacts with helpful, caring mentors will long be remembered. Help the child to make friends through social contacts and programs. Identify appropriate peers and constructive influences. Remember, your child does not always have to please you. And 6 equals friendly, but not having to please others.

Often, a young person who has a 6 tone in the Cycle I, will marry early. This impulse may be a desire to begin a family of one's own; however, it may also indicate the urge to leave home as soon as possible, perhaps to escape sociopathic patterns, domination, engulfment, or other dysfunction. Any cycle with the 6 tone highlights the relationship with family, spouse, ex-spouse, children (siblings) and/or parents and relatives. It is wise to use such times to make peace with one's family and friends. Later in life, such a cycle almost always emphasizes teaching, counseling, or interaction with groups. It is also a time for forming new friendships and harmonizing family relationships.

Tone 7 Cycles

The 7 tone, in any cycle, brings out the needs for specialized knowledge, meaning, self-understanding, life direction, spiritual identity, meditation, and reflection. Often, there is less contact with the everyday world. For a child who may experience the 7 tone in Cycle I, it is likely that he or she will spend more time in privacy, alone, removed from more mundane concerns. Sometimes, such a child is very quiet—at times almost invisible—preferring to receive nourishment from inner world sources of energy, study, and imagination that connect him or her to deep insights and wisdom. Such a child may find the inner world to be more real and sustaining than the outer. It is a time to encourage study, research, and the acquisition of knowledge.

I remember a wonderful little boy that I once counseled. He came to the office and remained largely nonverbal for fifteen minutes, as I searched for some connection that would draw him out. When I asked him if he ever did any writing or drawing, he suddenly replied that he was presently working on his novel about life under the ocean floor. He became much more animated when I asked if he might be willing to share a few chapters with me at our next meeting. He arrived the following week with a packet of papers. They contained several chapters and stories about the kingdom beneath the sea. He had also illustrated his writing beautifully. What a marvelous 9-year-old he was: talented, imaginative, almost from another world. His mother and teacher, who had been worried about his long silences and somewhat autistic behavior, then realized that he was just connected differently to another reality that in some way found its own entrance and harmony with the busy outer world. Thus, they found new ways not to disturb the 7 tone of contact with another dimension, while they also "helped him into the outer world." The key that bridged both realities for him was far more interior than anything outer or contemporary. In his own way, he was born out of his time. I believe many children (and adults) are like that today. They must try most of their lives to fit in where essentially they cannot.

Overall, the 7 tone in any cycle signals more time apart—a time for gaining knowledge, perhaps going back to school, reflecting, and finding the flow of one's life. It is less a time for busyness and outer involvement—more a time to draw back. A rhythm must be established that allows for contact and withdrawal—time spent with others and time spent apart and alone. Everyone needs some time alone, just to get to know oneself and to renew one's energies. But when the 7 tone is present strongly, a person may need more inward time for self-evaluation, reflection, prayer, meditation, and study. The 7 tone establishes the "God space and connection" within oneself. With deepened inner attunement, a person is then better able to return to the world and contribute in more meaningful ways. Two books that are especially meaningful for the 7 tone are *Disciplines of the Holy Quest*, by Flower A. Newhouse and *Ordinary People as Monks and Mystics*, by Marsha Sinetar.

Tone 8 Cycles

The 8 tone is a power tone. Themes of authority, control, position, management, property, and money are strong. The will power is extremely forceful. Even as a child, a person with the 8 tone in Cycle I will face issues centering around obedience, control, authority, mental domination, and power. The child likes to give orders. In some cases the child will become the wise parent of the parents, deciding what is best for them (usually quite accurately!) and how the household should be run. It is almost as if the child was born to parent his/her parents. Defiance and arguments may become more frequent if the adults behave childishly or foolishly, especially if they are weak and do not mean what they say. It is important for every child to have at least one area of control and responsibility. Let the child make some decisions. Find something for which the child can be in charge, such as a bank account, an allowance, a supervisory area, such as training a pet, cleaning up around the yard, setting the table, mowing the grass, etc. Find manageable ways to negotiate issues of will power, policy, capability, supervision, authority and boundaries. Provide options and assign rewards or consequences for choices made. Make it a win-win for everyone, is possible.

An 8 tone later on usually indicates connection with the corporate structure, business interests, the legal profession, and areas in society that center around justice and management. An 8 cycle is usually promising for financial gain and success in one's career. It is also a more dominant energy, which evokes powerful vibrations, decisiveness and the need to set appropriate limits and enforce policies.

Tone 9 Cycles

In any cycle a 9 tone suggests the "tide going out." It is a time for gaining through working with delays, surrendering to the larger process without martyring oneself, and being willing to serve the needs of others in one's midst. Interferences or challenges may crop up suddenly, such as an illness, a betrayal, or a disappointment. These difficulties are largely beyond one's own, personal control. Often, one's life opens up unexpectedly into contacts with strange people, different cultures, more expansive, geographical locations, and pressing, completely unexpected, areas of need, which require compassion, forgiveness and a large, generous perspective. It is a time to work for the greater good of the totality. Any 9 tone calls for surrender and compassionate response. Don't force anything. Pay whatever you owe to others.

In childhood the 9 tone often indicates a time of delay, almost like one's life being put on hold. Often, others' needs and demands may discourage personal gratification or advancement. The older child may have to care for younger siblings, or among parents and relatives, may need to be the mediator who keeps the peace in the home. Personal health issues may delay the natural flow of one's life. Sometimes, the child might seem to be forgotten, becoming almost an invisible child, at least for the time being. Later, a new emergence often occurs, bringing the desire to make up for lost time.

The 9 tone, in any cycle requires surrender to the immediate conditions and circumstances and a willingness to give of oneself, joyfully and freely. It often brings about enormous changes. Larger, more universal outcomes, are often beyond personal control or influence. In any 9 tone situation, look for areas of need and service to others, and give yourself to them. Try to maintain and embody your ideals. Let the river of life carry you forward without resisting its currents. Go with the flow. Work for the well-being of the totality, not just your own personal wishes.

PART II

INTERPRETING YOUR NAME

YOUR BIRTH CERTIFICATE NAME

Your name, as it appears on your birth certificate, describes the ways in which you are best advised to direct the energies contained in your birth triangle. Your original name, as recorded on your birth certificate, in ways that I cannot logically prove, seems to be a stronger, more lasting influence than that of other assumed names, married names, or nicknames, even if they are changed legally. It seems as if the original name carries its own mystical imprint and vibration, which describes a certain energy flow, leading each of us to our highest, most appropriate destiny in this lifetime. Whenever you change your name, you automatically activate secondary energy vibrations into your life path. Therefore, to change your name is an important decision, because the new name confronts the primary energies of your birth name. How interesting it is, as I have observed repeatedly, that people often change their names for conscious or unconscious intuitive needs. Upon investigation, it becomes clear that when each of us may wish to change our name, there is a deeper motivation and desire to activate a particular energy or tone in our energy field. Such a decision must be examined carefully. Considerable confusion may arise if a person changes names impulsively or too frequently. It is difficult to integrate too much variety. Try to avoid activating energies that may run counter to your deeper energy flow.

Basic Interpretation

I now want to explore several aspects of a person's name that can offer important clues about one's life path and purpose. So you can get a better understanding of the process of interpreting your name, I will use the fictitious name of John Peter Sellon as an example to show you the different stages of converting and then interpreting a name. There are four basic stages for determining the key energies represented in your name.

I. Converting your name into number energies. Use the following key to make the conversion.

Letters and Numbers.

1	2	3	4	5	6	7	8	9
a	b	c	d	e	f	g	h	i
j	k	l	m	n	o	p	q	r
s	t	u	v	w	x	y	z	

For example, the name John Peter Sellon would be converted as:

```
J O H N   P E T E R   S E L L O N
| | | |   | | | | |   | | | | | |
1 6 8 5   7 5 2 5 9   1 5 3 3 6 5
```

II. Determine what number energies appear most frequently and which do *not* appear in order to get a general sense and perspective of the energy vibrations of your name. These energies recurring most often indicate an intensity or concentration of power in a certain area. For example, many 5s may describe a life that is more kinetic, varied, physically active, and filled with changeable conditions and sudden reversals. In the name, John Peter Sellon, you will notice that the number 4 does not appear. Numerical energies that do not appear in a name often indicate abilities and sensitivities that need more effort to be externalized. These may be areas that require more attention in order to become balanced and integrated into the larger energy field. If such areas are also recessive in the birth triangle, it may be even more difficult to contact and express these energies. Look for them in other persons and learn from them.

III. Determine the numerical energy of each name by adding the corresponding numbers. The total must be below 10. If you add the totals and get a figure that is 10 or greater, reduce that number to a single digit by adding the double digits together. For example the individual names of John Peter Sellon reduces to 2, 1, 5 respectively as follows:

$$
\begin{array}{ccc}
\text{J O H N} & \text{P E T E R} & \text{S E L L O N} \\
1+6+8+5= & 7+5+2+5+9= & 1+5+3+3+6+5= \\
20 & 28 & 23 \\
2+0= & 2+8= & 2+3= \\
& 10 & \\
& 1+0= & \\
2 & 1 & 5
\end{array}
$$

In my research I have found that often the name totals indicate responses in life that people will require of you. Thus, the total of each of the three names will magnetize into activity certain themes that other people will need or ask of you. In the example, John Peter Sellon's numerical energies indicate the following:

John = 2 = closeness, supportiveness, detail
Peter = 1 = new ideas, courage
Sellon = 5 = fun, flexibility, variety

Such areas may or may not be those that are easy or natural for Mr. Sellon; but it is likely that they are being asked of him. A key principle to remember is that what we may not have received as a child may be the very talent or gift that we will need to give to others. Often, therefore, we must learn how to express those energies that were not stimulated or not healthfully developed in us during childhood. In some way or other, perhaps through contact with other informed persons, mentors, or classes, learn how to give to others what you may not have received yourself. Observe and talk to those who clearly manifest an energy area that you find difficult and may need to develop. Study lives that demonstrate what you might never have modeled as a child. At least become familiar enough with what seems strange to you, so that such themes and conditions will not defeat you. The following is a brief explanation of the energy you show the world.

What Do They Want from Me?

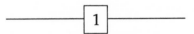

People look to you for original thinking, pioneer solutions, the cutting edge of new ideas and mental breakthroughs, self-starter attitudes, and autonomy. They expect verbal response.

People look to you for comfort, patience, sympathy, a listening ear, supportiveness, safety, handling details, cleaning up the mess, getting the facts, and the willingness to follow the leader.

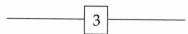

People look to you for joy, creativity, romance, color, and enthusiasm. They respond to your imagination.

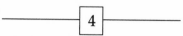

People look to you to be the dependable pillar, the one that always shows up and comes through. They want from you structure, good planning, reliable outcomes, and concrete results that are productive and useful.

People look to you for flexibility, fun, and adventure. They want physical involvement, interesting contact, and lots of variety. They like you to provide the excitement and stimulating good times. They love your playfulness and good humor.

People look to you for kindness, caring, and friendship. Learn to treat others like family. Volunteer some time for a constructive community cause.

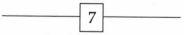

People look to you for knowledge and expertise. They want your wisdom and insight, your quiet and clear observations. Often, they expect perfection from you. They may look to you for deeper wisdom and knowledge in life.

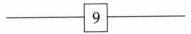

People look to you for your executive power and your authority to make the decisions and set the policies. They want you to take charge, especially in situations that involve finances, property, and business matters. Be clear on your boundaries.

—————| 9 |—————

People look to you for compassion, the larger perspective, mediation, and synthesis. You will be asked to make the best of some conditions that are even beyond your control. See the larger solutions in the midst of limitations, and move toward the greater possibilities.

YOUR DESTINY

The largest energy adjustment you will make in your life-time emerges as you move from birth force to destiny, or from the number at the bottom of your birth triangle to the number of your destiny, the total number derived from adding all of the numbers of your birth certificate name.

Numerically, your destiny emerges as the total of all the letter values of your birth certificate name. For example,

$$J + O + H + N \qquad P + E + T + E + R \qquad S + E + L + L + O + N$$
$$1 + 6 + 8 + 5 = \qquad 7 + 5 + 2 + 5 + 9 = \qquad 1 + 5 + 3 + 3 + 6 + 5 =$$
$$20 \qquad\qquad 28 \qquad\qquad\qquad 23$$
$$2 + 0 = \qquad\qquad 2 + 8 = \qquad\qquad\qquad 2 + 3 =$$
$$10$$
$$1 + 0 =$$
$$2 \qquad\qquad\qquad 1 \qquad\qquad\qquad\qquad 5$$

Destiny = 2 + 1 + 5 = **8**

Your destiny describes the primary purpose and focus of your lifetime. It is why you are here, and what you came to learn to be. Your destiny may or may not be what you might personally want (your heart's desire). Destiny is spiritual necessity for your highest, ultimate good. It is also a statement of the best you can do with what you have. Your destiny will reveal to you the greatest potential outcome—what will eventually produce the greatest overall fulfillment in your life. Destiny is deeper than your personality's cravings or impulses; it is of the soul, non-intrusive, yet all-embracing, and spiritually enhancing.

The following are suggestions for realizing fulfillment in each of the nine destiny tones.

Destiny 1

Learn to break free and stand on your own. Become autonomous through the power of your mind. Learn to take the initiative; know when to risk and move ahead with courage into the future possibility. Follow the open door of Providence; take advantage of new opportunities. Express your own independence, while also acknowledging others' views and opinions. Talk freely, but be present for others and learn from people by being a good listener. Take the time to nurture others who may not respond as quickly as you do. Avoid mental arrogance.

Destiny 2

Learn cooperation and patience. Be supportive and trustworthy; meet the other person's needs through sharing and closeness. Be available emotionally without becoming dependent or enabling. Feel intimacy and a close bond with another by being sensitive and anticipating needs. Gain necessary information and details. Build your confidence and address your own needs. Take care of yourself. Aim for equal partnership. Emotionally, learn how to be needed; subordination may bring ultimate gain.

Destiny 3

Learn to express your creativity and imagination through beauty, arts, and nature. Experience the joy of living; feel the romance of life. Find enjoyable ways to soar in consciousness, while remaining focused and grounded. Feel the glory of your dream and live it colorfully and dramatically. Experience upliftment through music, paintings, theater, poetry, stories, myths and legends, etc. Be in love with life; sing your song.

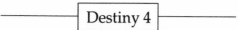

Destiny 4

Learn the value of achievement and accomplishment through hard work. Establish a foundation for your life; set your goals and develop a plan to achieve them. Follow through; be dependable, thorough and produce concrete results. But don't do others' work for them. Keep organized and live purposefully. In the midst of your labors, take time to rest and have some fun. Get the job done without being driven, rigid, or too serious. Steadfast efforts bring satisfaction and gain.

Destiny 5

Learn to be flexible and adaptable to continuous, often sudden, changes and surprises. Experience the incredible variety and spontaneity in life. Move your body, feel sensations, and gather the fruits of each moment as you travel. Accept new people as you find them, appreciating them for what they have to offer. Eat sensibly, exercise appropriately, and get your rest. Use humor to break up irritation or temper. Manage your moods. Diversify your interests. Keep many irons hot. Conserve your energy. Travel and experience life's many flavors. Smell the roses as you pass by! Expect the unexpected!

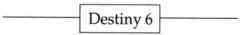

Destiny 6

Learn how to serve and nurture family, friends, and groups in society. Find ways to contribute constructively to the greater well-being of others. Deepen your friendships by appreciating people and caring for them. Help others to feel their own self-worth and to know that they are loved and lovable. Use your abilities in teaching, counseling, and entertaining to uplift those around you. In order to be liked and noticed by others, don't demean yourself or let your-self be taken in and used by people. Remain true to your own values and standards. Avoid just being a pleaser. Take care of yourself.

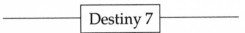

Destiny 7

Learn who you are! Gain depth and knowledge about life and your place in it. Establish your own inner connection with the Infinite. Live spiritually, according to the great cosmic laws of creation. Be true to your values and charac-ter. Take time to listen in the silence. Build strength from your quiet times of centering. Study and learn. Take time to be alone with your Maker. Avoid being aloof or elitist. Observe without being judgmental. In peace and serenity, sleep well each night.

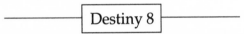

Destiny 8

Learn how to wield power and authority benevolently. In your decisions be fair and just. Become successful and prosperous in ways that empower others. Practice good stewardship. Establish clear boundaries and stand by them. Take charge of your life without dominating others. Resist tendencies toward greed, tyranny, and manipula-tion. Exercise control without becoming controlling. Aim for win-win.

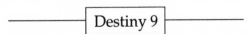

Destiny 9

Learn to express brotherhood, vision, and humanitarian service to the planet. Resolve unfinished business, forgive all, and release the past. Balance all relationships in the spirit of compassion. Do the best you can with whatever life gives you. Honor the needs of the totality ahead of personal feelings. Give of yourself without becoming a martyr or meddling, keeping others from their life lessons. Know when to enter in and when to stand back with love in your heart. You cannot save the world, but you can offer hope and a larger perspective to those you meet.

YOUR HEART'S DESIRE

Your heart's desire expresses what you would like to be, do, and accomplish. It describes how you would like your life to be. Your dream may or may not be in natural agreement with your destiny. Therefore, it is important to integrate the sense of what you want to do (your heart's desire) with the realization of what you came into this lifetime to become (your destiny). Help your heart's desire and your destiny work together as allies. Let your dream flow into your larger destiny and purpose. For example, a heart's desire of 6 (family, group, and friends) can work with the destiny of 1 (standing alone independently through individual thinking). You can find ways to be true to your own thinking while also being a good friend to others. Nurture others with your ideas. Find ways to help and to please that allow you to think for yourself.

You can find your heart's desire by adding the numerical value of the vowels in your full name. For example:

```
J  O  H  N     P  E  T  E  R     S  E  L  L  O  N
   6              5     5           5        6
6 + 5 + 5 + 5 + 6 = 27
2 + 7 = 9
```

The heart's desire for this fictional person is 9 (a desire to serve humanity).

If there are y's in your names, it will become clear that as you go forward in life these vibrations become more like vowels. Therefore, for each y in your name, add its numerical value (7) to your heart's desire. This crossover occurs more as your life progresses, usually appearing more noticeably from the late 30s onward.

For example, let's interpret the name Victor Yaeger Young:

V I C T O R   Y A E G E R   Y O U N G
  9   6   1 5   5   6 3
  9   6   **7** 1 5   5   **7** 6 3

Heart's Desire = 9 + 6 + 1 + 5 + 5 + 6 + 3 = 35 = **8**
Y Crossover = 9 + 6 + 7 + 1 + 5 + 5 + 7 + 6 + 3 = 49 = 13 = **4**

In this example, the heart's desire will change as the life progresses: the stronger desire for success and a dominant will power will move into the desire for concrete achievement and a willingness to do the required task (8 becomes 4).

Heart's Desire

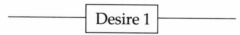

A desire to risk and be independent; a need for autonomy. A desire to learn and think toward the future.

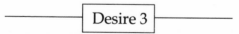

A desire to be close to another; a feeling of caution, neediness, and possible timidity. A desire for connection, emotional support, and communication.

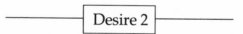

A desire to express oneself creatively with a strong imagination. A desire to live one's dream.

A desire for achievement and accomplishment. A desire for structure and usefulness.

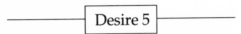

A desire for freedom, fun, and plenty of room for excitement and spontaneity. A need to experience continuous variety and newness.

A desire to be close to one's family, home and friends; the need for social contacts. A desire to be of service and to give and receive affection.

A desire to know and to learn; interest in study and a quest to experience the creator's mysteries. A desire for meaning and depth.

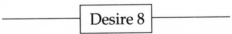

A desire for success, control and power; wanting to be in charge. A desire to manage others and to work in the name of a cause.

A desire to serve and be helpful to mankind; a need to give of self in ways that benefit the totality.

YOUR PERSONA

Your persona or "mask" is the way you come across to others; how others see you may or may not be the way you really are. The persona is also a kind of buffer or protection that empowers you to withstand the various demands and bombardments from the world around you. Your persona may mask the deeper motivations and intentions (your heart's desire and destiny), or it may resemble them quite closely. Without your persona, you have no boundaries; you expose yourself totally, like a sponge, to the onslaughts of the world.

The persona comes from the total of the numerical value of the consonants of your name. Here is our fictitious example again:

```
J  O  H  N    P  E  T  E  R    S  E  L  L  O  N
1     8  5    7     2     9    1     3  3     5
Persona = 1 + 8 + 5 + 7 + 2 + 9 + 1 + 3 + 3 + 5 = 44 = 8
```

The following are some characteristics of the nine personae.

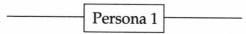

You come across to others as someone who is assured and independent.

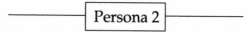

You come across to others as cautious, careful, perhaps timid, and hesitant.

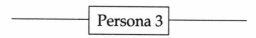

You seem very spacey and "floaty" to others—a colorful dreamer.

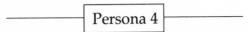

Persona 4

You seem like a rock of dependability and endurance. A worker who comes across as "straight" and reliable.

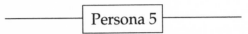

Persona 5

You seem like a free spirit—very zany and unconventional. You may seem like a gypsy and/or a clown.

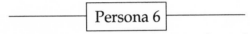

Persona 6

You seem friendly and warm—the "good guy" or "good girl." You seem to be a nurturer.

Persona 7

You seem private and reserved—the quiet observer.

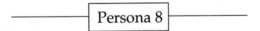

Persona 8

You seem to be the boss, dominant and in control.

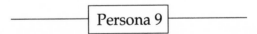

Persona 9

You seem to be self-giving and self-effacing, perhaps a very "nice" or colorless personality. You exude hope, idealism, and willingness, but you do this in ways that are not showy or pushy.

The total equation for understanding your name is now complete:

Heart's Desire + Persona = Destiny
Vowel Values + Consonant Values = Total Name

Try to integrate what you personally want (Heart's Desire) with what you are here to learn (Destiny). Your persona is how others often see you. It may or may not be like who you really are.

DOUBLE LETTERS: INTENSITIES (POCKETS) OF ENERGY

Double letters in a name indicate a concentration of energy, or a pressure which needs outlets. Without such outlets there is insufficient release, and the energy can bottle up and distort itself within a person, resulting in destructive and inappropriate behaviors.

Double 1 (aa, jj, ss)

You need to keep your mind stimulated and fulfilled, or you may tend to be a smart aleck or "wise guy" who comes across as a show-off and an egotist. Keep the mind active and diversified. Challenge the mind and release energy constructively. You think very quickly and are very verbal.

Double 2 (bb, kk, tt)

You may need emotional reassurance or there can be displays of worry, criticism, and obsessiveness over persons and details. Don't take it so personally. Replace fears with facts.

Double 3 (cc, ll, uu)

You have talent in the arts that needs to be released and explored. Keep creativity and imagination alive. Find outlets for beauty and romantic feelings.

Double 4 (dd, mm, vv)

You may have a tendency to overwork or to be rigid. You need good release into focused areas of achievement, such as a task to complete. Avoid drudgery or getting locked into a job.

Double 5 (ee, nn, ww)

You may have a tendency toward irritation and temper display, a possibility of lashing out or hitting something or somebody or using foul language to release tension and pressure. Sexual excess or addictive tendencies may become problems if energy is blocked. Watch out for frustration. Exercise regularly, see the humor in life, and get some sleep.

Double 6 (ff, oo, xx)

You may show an extra involvement within family or social ties, issues in marriage and home, enmeshment from early childhood. Nurture and appreciate others. Avoid sociopathic tendencies.

Double 7 (gg, pp, yy)

You may be involved in specialized research or deeper, concentrated knowledge within a certain area. Practice meditation in some form. Avoid too much abstraction or arrogant, elitist tendencies.

Double 8 (hh, qq, zz)

You may exhibit mental dominance and a forceful will power that must manage and be in control of others. Manage some area without dominating, condemning, or suppressing others. Overcome tendencies to be judgmental.

Double 9 (ii, rr)

You give extra service to others. Clear up unseen, unexpected old business. Cope willingly with circumstances and demands beyond your control and personal wishes. Let compassion and forgiveness empower a need that may seem extreme or unpleasant.

For example the names Debbie, Melissa, and Vannella:

D   E   **B**   **B**   I   E
4 + 5 + **2** + **2** + 9 + 5 = 27 = 9

The 9 gives humanitarian tendencies, and the double 2 stimulates personal concerns, needs, and possible criticisms or worries about those most loved and needed.

M   E   L   I   **S**   **S**   A
4 + 5 + 3 + 9 + **1** + **1** + 1 = 24 = 6

The 6 gives friendliness, but the double 1 may bring a streak of ornery assertiveness and an extra need to be verbally assertive and independent.

V   A   **N**   **N**   E   **L**   **L**   A
4 + 1 + **5** + **5** + 5 + **3** + **3** + 1 = 27 = 9

The 9 gives compassion and humanitarianism, with the double 5 expressing a need for physical release, possible temper, and itchy, free spirit behaviors. The double 3 demands an artistic self-expression.

THE PLANES OF EXPRESSION

The planes of expression describe numerical "tones" of behaviors—the ways that life energy comes out of you through your body, emotions and mind, and the attitudes you express toward physical, emotional mental, and intuitive areas of your life. To find the vibration of your physical plane, count the quantity of 4s and 5s in your total name. For your emotional plane, count the quantities of 2s, 3s and 6s. For the mental tone, count the quantities of 1s and 8s. For the intuitive tone, count the quantities of 7s and 9s.

Physical Plane

The tone of your physical plane describes how you release energy through your own body, how you relate physically to others, and how you see your physical environment.

To find the tone of the physical plane, simply count the quantity (not the numerical value) of 4s and 5s in the total name. For this fictitious person, there are five 5s and no 4s.

J	O	H	N	P	E	T	E	R	S	E	L	L	O	N
1	6	8	**5**	7	**5**	2	**5**	9	1	**5**	3	3	6	**5**

There are no 4s, but five 5s mean that the tone of his physical plane is 5. Mr. Sellon would need to move around frequently and experience many new sensations in life. He may be quite sexual and physical in his relationships.

The following are characteristics of people with each of the nine numerical tones expressed on the physical plane.

──────────┤ 1 ├──────────

You relate to the physical plane more through ideas and concepts. For example, you might *think* of cleaning the house or *see* it cleaned before you actually clean it. You might see something to be done and tell others to do it. You want things to happen quickly.

You are somewhat shy and very particular about your body. You need to be cautious about any kind of daredevil behaviors. You favor security and safety. Physically, you need protection. You need a safe place and someone close, physically, to fill your lonely hours. You like to share tasks. You express communication best through continuous physical contact and close proximity. You may worry when you are alone. Physically, you may cling and nag too much. You need to feel close emotionally to the person with whom you share your body.

You are quite spacey and unfocused and possibly not too well organized in your physical environment. You may tend to dream along over life's details. You may not always feel grounded. You like beauty around you. Romance is connected more to the aesthetics of your surroundings, such as living near the ocean or in the beauty of nature. You may not be well organized or attentive to details.

You want results and hard work to come from those around you and the environment. You want regularity and structure. You look for practical outcomes. You value achievement. You expect every day to be organized.

---| 5 |---

You move quickly from place to place. You like physical contact and kinetic excitement. You need frequent change to keep you excited. You might bump into things. Watch your speed! Keep focused if you hurry. Avoid sexual excesses, extreme appetites, temper eruptions, or abusive reactions. Get rest before you exhaust yourself. Sports may be a regular part of your life.

---| 6 |---

You like a friendly, family feeling in your physical environment. You like people to be around you. You do for those you like. Your home is your castle and comfort. You may be casual in the way you stay organized. You nurture others, and you entertain them. You may be very chatty. Avoid gossiping about others; your conversations may cause echoes.

---| 7 |---

You are a perfectionist who must have everything in total order around you. You dislike sloppiness and dirty messes. Your creed is "It always has to be right." You scrutinize the environment. You can't stand clutter. You may also be quite private about your body. You seek knowledge about what concerns you deeply.

---| 8 |---

You must dominate and make the decisions. You want to be successful and live well on the physical plane. You want to be in control. Avoid aggressive, bullying tendencies. Share the wealth! Empower others, rather than be jealous or demeaning. You may be ruthless with the opposition, but it's better to be patient and forgiving.

$$\boxed{9}$$

You live more out of the physical world than in it. You might forget details and sequences easily. Sometimes what is directly in front of you may seem invisible. Remember to connect with and care for your physical body. Come into your body and environment. Don't assume anything. Remember what is close to you. Work through continuous delays, outside interferences and disappointments. Keep moving forward.

Emotional Plane

The tone of your emotional plane indicates how you release energy though your emotions and how you relate to others emotionally.

To find the emotional tone of a name, count the *quantity* of 2s, 3s, and 6s. Here is our fictional person who has a total of 5 of these numbers.

J	O	H	N	P	E	T	E	R	S	E	L	L	O	N
1	**6**	8	5	7	5	**2**	5	9	1	5	**3**	**3**	**6**	5

Five 2s, 3s, and 6s mean that the tone of Mr. Sellon's emotional plane is 5. He might have many mood swings. He needs to find nonviolent, physical outlets for his emotions. His emotions may change frequently, like a yo-yo, if he feels fenced in. He needs space emotionally.

The following are characteristics of people with each of the nine tones as expressed on the emotional plane.

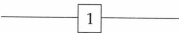

Rather than emoting directly, you may prefer to talk about your feelings, perhaps intellectualizing them, distilling and abstracting verbally from your emotional responses. You relate to others emotionally by verbalizing your ideas and concepts. You are often "post-emotional," perhaps contacting your feelings by talking about them. You may become quite passionate about your views.

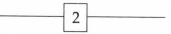

You are needy emotionally. You want closeness and personal involvement from another person whom you trust. You are very selective emotionally—about people, places, situations, and events. You tend to particularize and take others' responses very personally. You need to feel that the person(s) you care about are always near you or at your side—within reach. You may worry a lot. You must feel connected to someone. You feel life's cameos and nuances. Avoid being critical, especially when you feel attacked. You don't have to react defensively. Replace your fears by getting the facts. Share your concerns with someone you trust. You probably prefer one-on-one relationships over group activities.

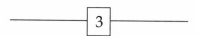

Emotionally, you are a romantic. You "space out" easily and enter your own world of imagination and fantasy, especially if the going gets too tough or the demands are too great. You may be quite histrionic. You feel dramatically. You may not always view your loves accurately or realistically.

You take a problem-solving approach to emotions. Rather than spending a lot of time "feeling" with someone else, you look for what needs to be done. You may feel that just emoting is a waste of valuable time. You may come across to others emotionally as rather "straight vanilla" and perhaps cold and one-dimensional. When others need you to be emotionally available or sensitive, you may respond more pragmatically or in a dry-toned, emotionless manner. Your affect may be somewhat flat. You often show love by doing for others without demonstrating your feelings. Value others for themselves, not just for their productivity.

You are very restless emotionally. Sometimes your mood swings are like thundershowers—a brief, noisy storm, then the sunshine returns. You may want to release emotionally through your body—viscerally, sexually, and kinetically. Swimming or kicking a ball might be helpful. You are very "up and down" emotionally, and at times you may feel "itchy," panicky, confined, and claustrophobic. Exercise relieves irritable "itchy" moods. You may erupt suddenly, although usually not for too long at one time. Discharge energy constructively when it has bottled up inside you. Your sudden need for space and freedom may make you seem cold or fickle toward others.

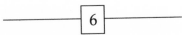

You need much appreciation and many emotional strokes from others. You like affection and warmth. Friends can give you positive reinforcement. You direct much emotional energy toward family and friends. Be true to your feelings. Avoid pleasing others in order to be popular or accepted. You must be noticed. Develop better self-esteem; don't depend on others' opinions or on status for your self-worth.

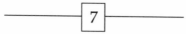

You are very private emotionally, preferring to work out your feelings reflectively, from the interior, meditative, analytical perspective. Sometimes, enjoyable reading can release feelings in you. You feel quietly and deeply. Learn to be emotionally accessible. Share your feelings and inner processes with others. Come into the world emotionally.

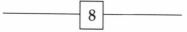

You are very controlled emotionally. You dislike excessive emotional display, and you try to keep a lid on others' responses. You may become superrational or judgmental in your evaluation of individuals and situations. Try to allow others to express their feelings. Avoid suppressing others' emotions. You don't have to be vengeful or retaliatory.

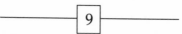

You are highly idealistic and tend to release your emotions in your concerns for others. You may not attend to your own emotional needs. You may, through empathy, create your own picture of what is happening. Your feelings may be grandiose. Feel closely and particularly, not jut universally or impersonally.

Mental Plane

The tone of your mental plane identifies how you release energy through your mind and thinking.

To find the tone of the mental plane, count the quantity of 1s and 8s in the total name. Our fictitious person has a total of three 1s and 8s.

J	O	H	N		P	E	T	E	R		S	E	L	L	O	N
1	6	**8**	5		7	5	2	5	9		**1**	5	3	3	6	5

Three 1s and 8s mean that the tone of Mr. Sellon's mental plane is 3. He has a very creative, imaginative mind, perhaps at times a bit unrealistic, unfocused, or impractical. He may dream often of a creative fantasy, an enchanting scene, feeling, or relationship. He may not want to focus on the "reality" of the situation.

The following are characteristics of people with each of the nine tones as they are expressed on the mental plane.

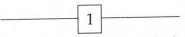

You have a catalytic mind that receives flashes of new ideas and possibilities. You think very quickly and need to keep your mind stimulated and interested. You are easily bored. Record your ideas before they fly out of your mind. Verbalize, talk with those who inspire you.

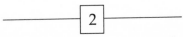

You may be shy or selective about expressing your ideas to others. You must trust another deeply before opening up about how you think. You fear others' rejection of your own thoughts. You see the little things very clearly but may not see the big picture. You may get bogged down in details. You need others' support and encouragement to develop confidence in your own thinking. You are aware of what is intricate and minute. You are highly selective, perhaps critical.

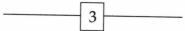

You have a very imaginative, inventive mind that colors people and events according to how you see them. You may not always think sequentially but in spots and echoes of color and romanticized feeling. The arts stimulate your thinking. Distinguish between others' responses and your own interpretation of them. You can easily visualize your dreams and desires. You may "space out" mentally if you don't want to look at situations and others' needs.

You think practically. You like ideas and plans that work. You don't like to explore or theorize mentally. You believe, "What you see is what you've got." You are a realist and like concreteness. Your mind responds best to what is useful and workable. You may scorn any "pie in the sky" theories or fantasies. You often think about the task before you.

You have an exploratory mind; you may be into many different areas of curiosity and interest. Touching upon many fields of learning and information, you try to keep current and do well to focus your many interests toward some common center. Keep all the irons in your fire hot. Be sure to consider your body's needs. You can easily get ahead of yourself. Yet, you can bring many convergent ideas into a flash of insight or sudden discovery.

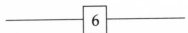

You tend to express thoughts that others want to hear. Often you are influenced by the responses of family and relatives, or your peers, rather than thinking for yourself and standing up for your own ideas. You need the support of others in order to express your own thoughts. You may repeat others' views. Get beyond gossip. Be authentic! Community needs and teaching may interest you.

You have a very deeply focused and specialized mind. Often you go into a deep study of a certain area of knowledge, perhaps becoming an expert in your chosen field. You can see through others immediately, and you know where they are really coming from. You do not have much patience with those who are ignorant or uninformed. You penetrate what you observe. You can be demanding, even aloof, especially when you are preoccupied with study or a project.

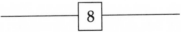

You try to control others' thinking. You must be right all the time, and you might relate conversation and ideas to business and investments. You are quite dominant mentally toward others. Empower others with your managerial mind. Allow them to have their own views and opinions. You don't have to change others. As you supervise, back off.

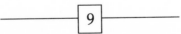

Your ideas are very idealistic, humanitarian, and perhaps a bit unreal in the practical sense. You think synthetically, in terms of a lofty vision that is possible for all humankind.

Intuitive Plane

The tone of your intuitive plane expresses the rhythms and interplay of your daily life with your interior self and its connections with the energies of the Infinite.

To find the tone of the intuitive plane, count the quantity of 7s and 9s in the total name. Our example has a total of two 7s and 9s.

J	O	H	N		P	E	T	E	R		S	E	L	L	O	N
1	6	8	5		**7**	5	2	5	**9**		1	5	3	3	6	5

Two 7s and 9s mean that Mr. Sellon's intuitive tone is 2. He tunes into his intuitive awareness best when he is in close company with a loved one or working with data. His intuition flows best when he is with someone that he trusts.

Here are characteristics of people with each of the nine tones as they are expressed on the intuitive plane.

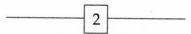

Your intuitions emerge quickly, especially when your mind is actively involved in new ideas and new possibilities. Keep reading, talking, and learning.

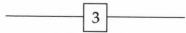

Your intuitions surface in quiet places where there is peace, security, and a feeling of intimacy. Data and details stimulate insights.

Your intuition is greatly stimulated by beauty: lovely music, poetry, colors, nature, and romance.

Your intuition becomes active as you are working on a task. While doing a project, your mind may give you deeper intuitive insights that arise from your soul's receptivity.

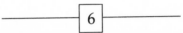

While on the move, your intuition speaks to you quickly, in the moment. If you take a trip, the change and variety spark your intuitions. New acquaintances and changes bring new insights.

Your intuition speaks to you when you are with friends and people. Affection for friends and family stimulates deeper realizations. The group feeds you and reveals deeper dimensions in you.

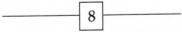

In privacy and quiet your deeper self speaks to you. In cloistered places and in solitude you find deeper meaning for your life and are better able to see into events and experience.

Intuition may surface while you are involved in your business or while managing a project. Once you have made up your mind, nobody can change or dissuade your thinking.

--------------------| 9 |--------------------

Intuition comes to you as you reflect on the possibilities for brotherhood and compassionate service to humanity. Emptying yourself in service, light fills you.

It is extremely important to consider your planes of expression. The tonalities of your physical, emotional, mental, and intuitive energies will affect your relationships and your decisions. Your planes of expression can also help you to understand where others are coming from as they respond to you. (See Table 3 on p. 112 for a summary of the characteristics manifested by each of the nine tones on the four planes of expression.)

Most importantly, it is obvious that each person is at least four-dimensional. The various tones of the planes of expression are interacting in a person simultaneously and holistically at four different levels. What a person is on the physical plane, tonally, may not be at all like what the same individual is emotionally. For example, a human being may be very dominant physically (8), but at the same time may be quite needy emotionally (2). Or, a person may be quite practical mentally (4), while being somewhat reckless and unorganized physically (5). An individual may not be equally mature or consistent on each of the different planes of expression. In a relationship it is always wise to compare the planes of expression to see where the individuals may be very similar, opposite, or complementary. The planes of expression go far in identifying and clarifying issues that are likely to surface in a relationship; they may indicate dissonances that must either be modified or accepted in order for any deeper coherence and bonding to occur.

Table 3. The Tones of the Planes of Expression.

Tone	Physical	Emotional	Mental	Intuitive
1	Relates to physical environment more through the mind and ideas (abstract).	Post-emotional; processes by talking about feelings more than displaying them at the time.	Gets very quick, catalytic ideas; needs to write them down.	Gets insights while reading, talking, and thinking.
2	Gentle and cautious about the body; not aggressive or violent; precise and supportive; follows the lead.	Needs close contact; wants attention and to feel OK; sympathizes; needs to be in touch.	Cautious and shy about sharing ideas; needs encouragement in their thinking.	Insights come in the midst of intimacy and quiet closeness.
3	Not organized; more in the moment and proceeding by inspiration and imagination; can space out easily.	Responds to the romantic and beautiful; can easily fantasize/dream and imagine what is not.	Colors ideas and thoughts according to own imagination; creative thinker.	Inspiration comes from romance and the arts.
4	Proceeds by organization and planning; wants results; needs structure and schedules; enjoys goals; feels good when productive; step by step hard work yields good outcome.	Cut and dry; approaches feelings as a problem solver; prefers to approach feeling by doing; doesn't waste time.	Practical thinker; interested in ideas that work and are useful; values the "bottom line"; relates ideas to work; pragmatic realist.	Gets inspiration and insight while on task or working and planning.
5	Highly kinetic; needs much movement, variety and physical contact; needs to release through exercise, sports,	Like a thunderstorm; mood swings are frequent; often physical when feeling emo-	Curious about many areas; likes new ideas; flexible and adaptable to change; can	Gets insights when moving, driving, traveling, or doing

Table 3. The Tones of the Planes of Expression (cont.).

Tone	Physical	Emotional	Mental	Intuitive
5 (cont)	and visceral discharge; cannot sit still for long; meets different persons easily; doesn't often finish tasks.	tionally tense or stressed; easily restless and irritable; needs freedom and open space for release.	roll with the punches; can balance many different projects at once.	several things at once.
6	Likes a warm, friendly, homey, family environment; enjoys social contacts and company; affectionate; seeks a group.	Friendly; needs appreciation and approval; likes "strokes" or acknowledgment; needs to be included and noticed.	Tends to think as peers do; needs approval; helpful toward others.	Gains insight from social service and friends.
7	Perfectionistic about order and cleanliness; sometimes abstract and private; may not easily enter into mainstream; reserved about the body.	Private emotionally; does not like to show emotions; processes feelings inside or through analytical thinking about the feelings.	Specialized mind, good researcher; seeks knowledge and depth of perception; laser penetration.	Gains insight from meditation and study.
8	Must control; wants to make the decisions; power oriented; good manager; takes charge; strong-willed; wants success.	Controlled and controlling emotionally; does not like showiness of feelings.	Tries to control what others think; strongly managerial; dominant; thinks he/she is right.	Mind is made up; insights and money are linked.
9	Lives out of intuitive feelings and is not often aware of the physical plane; floats like a balloon over the world.	Highly idealistic and general in feelings; assumes the best about others.	Universal scope of feeling and compassion.	Insights come from service.

PART III

COUNSELING
AND
NUMERICS

VARIED RHYTHMS

In order to use Pythagorean numerics as a counseling tool, it is helpful to get as large a perspective as possible. Several people with a similar problem may each handle it differently. WHERE DOES THE ENERGY WANT TO GO? Try to arrange the various pieces of data, previously discussed, in a way that is clear visually. You will then discover that certain concrete information will begin to awaken a larger, intuitive response. The energies and positions of the various numerical tonalities will do their dance in front of you, and you can make important associations and discoveries from the mix and clustering of the variables. Ask your client questions and dialogue with others to clarify and validate your insights and hunches. Very often, you can sense tendencies and more appropriate ways to handle a particular issue that is challenging a person. You can become sensitive to different options and choices that are available. You can find together the "clear stream" and the open door that frees the energy and allows for the most sensible and wise solution.

Balance rarely comes from equal proportions; rather, it emerges from the ability to identify and coordinate variables. Pythagorean numerics describe a person's moving energy field by suggesting how different temperaments, tones of thought, feelings and activities are interacting in the soul's company. Particular energies in individuals can operate on their own, or in cooperation with the others, to the benefit and well-being of the larger, total organism. Thus, as a microcosm of its own, each person's energies mix and move in their own spaces, while at the same time they also resonate with many other lives that are also vibrating in their own ways throughout the planet.

In beginning to feel the dance of energies mingling within ourselves and others, we can sense the dynamic ways that different lives can influence each other.

Pythagorean numerics describe the varied rhythms and energies of every individual and suggest an unlimited spectrum of possibilities for communication and contact between people. All lives are magnetic and affect each other: as different intentionalities and temperaments in human beings respond to particular times and situations, many energies of life can interact to provide the most appropriate personal and communal expression and creative outcome. The more sensitively and subtly individuals can feel and direct their energies, the more successful their life and relationships can become, and the more all lives benefit. Thus, Pythagorean numerics help indicate what is most harmonious for an individual; they reveal multiple options for the greater well-being of all those who may be involved. What any single individual does, feels, and thinks affects everyone for better or for worse. We are all interconnected.

Pythagorean numerics is an approach to one's life that can identify patterns of cause and effect—choices and consequences. In total, Pythagorean numerics is not a quick fix or an easy answer, but a beautiful way of helping individuals to feel their energies and direct them toward the most healthy and appropriate outcome. Pythagorean numerics is not a reading or a future prediction; it is a window into seeing tendencies in one's life, understanding the various options for responding, and learning to direct energy now toward what needs balance and creative overcoming. Also, such an approach can show patterns moving us toward greater life purpose and fulfillment.

Finally, Pythagorean numerics also offers hints of a wondrous synchronicity—times of surprising convergence, when from unexpected sources our life experiences the contact and mysterious blessings and leadings from the unknown. Pythagorean numerics is, therefore, another tool for finding one's larger purpose and life direction in God, and is in this way a gateway into sources of inspiration and illumination: a moment by moment process that leads to larger spiritual fulfillment.

SETTING UP A CHART AND FORMAT FOR COUNSELING

Through the years I and my associates have developed a visual Life Path Inventory that presents clearly and effectively the necessary data which this book has just identified and described. In addition, a computer print-out is available for both children and adults. A one-on-one consultation is even more effective and holistic, offering insights through sympathetic resonance and dialogue shared together.

Since the birthdate describes the energies we bring into a particular lifetime, I like to begin with this information. The energies of the birthdate descend into the personality and manifest through the name on the birth certificate. Visually, such a chart might look like figure 8 on p. 122. Another visual approach and organization of data is figure 9 on p. 125. We are using a fictitious example in figures.

Counseling Guidelines

▼ What is the **Birth Force Tone** (the number at the base of the triangle)?

▼ What is the **Day of Birth Tone**?

▼ How can these two tones best work together? (Integrate.)

▼ What is the spread and the variety of energies that our fictitious Brenda brings into this lifetime?

▼ What energies are more dominant? Which is recessive? Notice **Tonalities**.

▼ What are the **Cycles**? Note crucial years and identify crossover themes and energies that may occur as one cycle moves into another.

▼ What is the flow of Brenda's life path throughout the four cycles?

▼ How will the energy of the triangle be directed through the name?

▼ How is Brenda's energy moving?

▼ What is Brenda's **Destiny**—what did she come to accomplish?

▼ How does this agree or conflict with her **Heart's Desire** or with what Brenda personally may want?

▼ What, if any, integration is required to move from Birth Force to Destiny?

▼ Are there bottlenecks of energy? Note double letters and their appropriate tones.

▼ How can Brenda release these energy clusters creatively and constructively?

▼ How does Brenda come across to others—what tone is her **Persona**?

▼ How might Brenda tend to function **physically, emotionally, mentally and intuitively**?

▼ Is Brenda more odd or even? Where is she odd or even?

▼ What kind of relationship would Brenda most likely seek and/or need?

▼ Compare her **Planes of Expression** with someone else's! (Relationships.)

▼ What jobs or areas of work would seem most appropriate for Brenda?

▼ What might Brenda be more independent; where may she be more needy?

▼ Identify abilities and likely trouble spots.

▼ What is Brenda's life dream—her sense of who she is and where she wants to go?

Let's use the counseling guidelines to interpret Brenda's energy.

First, get an overview of the numerical energies within the triangle. (Remain nonjudgmental.) Notice the birth force energy 3 and the birth day 5. Integrate these energies: Brenda would naturally have a creative, artistic tendency (3), which would most likely be expressed physically through the body and its movements (5). This artistic-physical energy would be supported by a very keen mind (1:4) that can coordinate and organize mentally whatever is happening—when she has to! The 4:0 indicates that she may not *naturally* be organized herself. However, you can see in the Heart's Desire (4) that Brenda *wants* to achieve results and be more organized. So she would most likely want to develop this recessive 4 energy. (4:0 → 4 Heart's Desire).

Brenda's cycles are 1, 7, 8, and 7. Until 33 years of age, she will be working out independence through the mind. She will be learning how to stand on her own two feet. The 1 cycle combines with her 1:4 energy in the triangle, thus indicating good opportunities through use of mental, pioneering energy. She needs learning and education.

The 7 energy in the triangle has the tone of 1 (7:1), so there would be a certain specialized, scientific, psychological, spiritual sensitivity in the midst of the mental activity. The second cycle (years 34–43) shows a 7 tone, so this might be a time when Brenda would deepen her knowledge and expertise in a specific field of study. Brenda's specific 1, 3, 5, and 7 energies might combine to yield work in the health field, or perhaps in an area such as journalism or illustration.

It would be helpful for Brenda to take some workshops or classes in social interaction, motivational planning, and time management. She'd be wise to fill in the –4, –6, and –8 energies. She may go back to school.

Next, relate the birth force and energies within the triangle to the name. Brenda's name pattern is 4-1-5. She comes in more odd than even, and she remains odd with a Destiny of 5. Thus, her life path will most likely be more filled with changes and variety, not very predictable or structured. She may change jobs and/or relationships often. Her life needs variety and excitement. Her Heart's Desire shows that Brenda wants to be organized and produce concrete results 4. She has an independent persona 1,

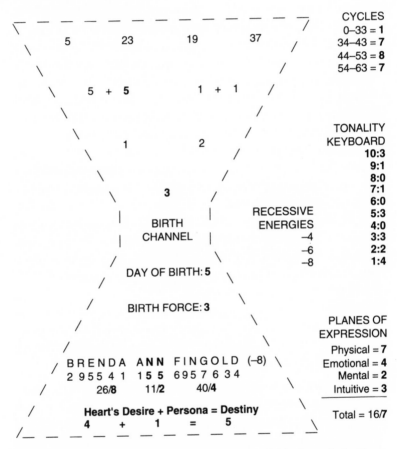

Figure 8. An example of the hourglass of birth and destiny chart—another visual approach to analyzing energy–data using the name Brenda Ann Fingold. With these data we are able to get a clearer picture of the forces working in Brenda's life (see the Counseling Guidelines on pages 119–120).

giving others the idea that she is a free thinker, needing autonomy. The Destiny 5 shows that Brenda will have many different impressions and experiences. She is a free spirit, and most likely will meet many different persons and situations. It would be helpful for the dialogue between structure 4 and freedom 5 to be worked out in some agreeable way within Brenda. She would feel better if she were able to work out some specific areas of definite planning and organization. Notice also the 7 on the physical plane, which indicates a perfectionistic tendency in certain areas that are important to Brenda. Thus, Brenda could be very casual, even sloppy, in some areas, while becoming meticulous and very ordered in others. This is part of the paradox in every individual. Brenda may be much more of a free spirit in the overall sense, yet she may be fastidious in certain details. Energy finds its own ways to move through complexity.

Emotionally, Brenda shows a 4 tone; she may be quite a romantic and show artistic tendencies, yet emotionally, she may respond somewhat "straight" and prefer to work through the feelings in a more dry, problem-solving way. She may be shy about sharing her ideas and feelings with a mental 2. She would need to have the facts together, and she would have to feel close to the person with whom she is sharing. Sometimes, although her mind is active and alert, she may feel caution about revealing her thoughts. She needs someone else's encouragement and support in order to gain confidence. Intuitively, the tone is 3 which indicates that Brenda feels her deepest moments when she is involved in something creative and artistic. Playing music, dancing, being in nature, writing, etc., helps to release deeper, intuitive insights. She needs to express herself artistically (3:3), and her intuitive 3 tone links with her birthforce (3). In her heart she is a romantic, but may find it difficult to share these feelings emotionally.

The totals of the three names, Brenda Ann Fingold, are 8, 2, and 4. Therefore, it is likely that others will look to Brenda for some areas that do not come naturally to her: taking charge (8), close sensitivity and emotional support (2), and dependability and structure (4).

The double N (55) may indicate a certain restlessness in Brenda. She needs to exercise and move around, especially when she is feeling pressure and stress. Swimming and dancing might be especially helpful in dealing with irritability and feelings of confinement. Her movements may need refinement given her physical plane is 7.

Thus, from the information that is available in the triangle and name, it is clear that Brenda Ann Fingold is a person with considerable creative and artistic talent. She likes freedom, and she is a romantic with her own ideas. It is more difficult for her to fit into groups, structures, and belief systems. She gets her own stream of creative, intuitive insights and direction. Her movement may not be steady and gradual. She tends to live more in the moment, and often may not follow through in obvious, organized methods. She shows depth as well as variety, but her agenda is not naturally sequential. She achieves results from spontaneous meetings with many different persons. She wants to be dependable, and will be more so as she moves into her third cycle 8. In relationships, Brenda would be wise to be close to someone more organized and stable, yet who also is fun-loving, flexible, and not possessive. The person should also have an appreciation for the arts and nature. It would be helpful if such an individual could be emotionally supportive of Brenda's ideas and creative ventures, yet not need a great deal of sympathy or emotional attention in return because her emotional tone (4) suggests her affect may be somewhat flat.

BIRTH DATA:

Birth Triangle   Cycles

_____ _____ _____   I _____ _____

_____ _____ _____   II _____ _____

_____ _____   III _____ _____

Birth Force: _____   IV _____ _____

Tonalities

1 _____ 2 _____ 3 _____

4 _____ 5 _____ 6 _____ Recessive Energies: _____

7 _____ 8 _____ 9 _____

BIRTH CERTIFICATE NAME:

Name: First_____ Middle_____ Last_____

_____   _____   _____

_____   _____   _____

Name Totals: _____   _____   _____

Recessive Energies:_____

Planes of Expression: Physical _____ Emotional _____

Mental _____ Intuitive _____

Heart's Desire: _____ + Persona _____ = Destiny _____

Y Transition: _____ + Persona _____ = Destiny _____

Figure 9. A visual approach to organize and analyze energy data.

Counseling Guidelines Worksheet

What is the Birth Force Tone (the number at the base of the triangle) ? _____

What is the Day of Birth Tone? _____

How can these two tones best work together (integrate)?

_____

_____

_____

_____

What is the variety of energies this person brings into this lifetime? _____

_____

_____

_____

_____

What energies are more dominant? Which are recessive? (Notice tonalities.)_____

_____

_____

What are the Cycles? (Note crucial years and identify crossover themes and energies that may occur once one cycle moves into another.)_____

_____

_____

_____

What is the flow of the life path throughout the four cycles?

_____

How will the energy of the triangle be directed through the name?_____

_____

How is the energy moving?_____

_____

What is the Destiny? What needs to be accomplished?____

_____

_____

How does this agree or conflict with Heart's Desire or with what he or she personally may want?_____

_____

_____

_____

What, if any, integration is required to move from Birth Force to Destiny?_____

_____

_____

Are there bottlenecks of energy? (Note double letters and their appropriate tones.)_____

_____

How can energy clusters be released creatively and constructively?_____

_____

_____

How does _____ come across to others—what tone is the Persona?_____

_____

How might _____ tend to function physically, emotionally, mentally and intuitively?_____

_____

_____

_____

More odd or even?_____

Where is _____ odd or even?_____

What kind of relationship is sought or needed?_____

_____

_____

How do the Planes of Expression compare with the other people in life?_____

_____

_____

What jobs or areas of work would seem most appropriate?

_____

_____

Where is independence; shown by what number? Needy? Shown by what?_____

_____

_____

What are abilities and trouble spots?_____

_____

_____

What is the life dream or goal?_____

_____

_____

HARMONIES AND IMBALANCES WITHIN THE TEMPERAMENT

Pythagorean numerics offer clear indicators of areas within the personality that are either balanced or unbalanced. As a general guideline, look for what is well-developed as well as those areas that are either underdeveloped or excessively overemphasized. A missing number, either in the birth triangle and/or the name, may indicate an energy that is recessive or underdeveloped. A recessive energy identifies an important need that must be brought forth and blended into a person's larger pattern. The following are suggested areas to develop for each of the nine recessive energies.

Recessive 1

Exercise more mental power and daring; become a self-starter. (Will involve persons born after 2000 A.D. as before the year 2000 it is almost impossible not to have at least one number 1 when considering your birth data.)

Recessive 2

Develop sympathy, closeness and supportiveness. Overcome fears and worries with facts. Overcome fears of rejection. Establish intimacy with some trusted person or pet. Stop playing the victim.

Recessive 3

Cultivate more creativity, beauty and color in life. Try more "free flow" experiences. Find outlets for artistic self-expression. Live the dream.

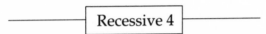

Structure, plan and organize. Set definite goals to achieve. Follow through; be dependable and committed.

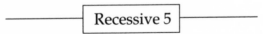

Be more flexible. Seek variety and physical contact. Release rigidity. Play more and have some fun in life.

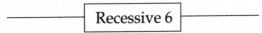

Encourage social responsibility, group consciousness, and family home warmth. Nurture others through service. Overcome anti-social or sociopathic attitudes toward society. Contribute to the community (volunteer).

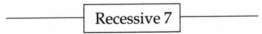

Develop inner depth, awareness of spiritual laws, life purpose, and meaning. Study, meditate and reflect. Spend more time alone.

Take charge of situations and own life. Set limits and follow through on them.

Demonstrate humanitarian concern, empathy, and compassion. Practice forgiveness and brotherhood. Consider the well-being of the greater totality.

Just as there can be recessive energies, there may also be overdeveloped or excessive energies. Dominant energies can lead to difficulties such as addictions, bizarre behaviors and obsessions. If we are aware of these tendencies, we can work toward channeling this energy in positive ways.

———————| Excessive 1 |———————

The tendency is to be egocentric, mentally narcissistic, and overly self-important. Try to be more patient with others and more receptive to their ideas.

———————| Excessive 2 |———————

The tendency is to be fearful, hypercritical, obsessive about details, and/or overly possessive. Reduce your paranoia, stress and worry by not taking everything too personally.

———————| Excessive 3 |———————

May tend to live in a dreamworld and come across as naive, fickle or histrionic. Strive to keep your feet on the ground—be more realistic and less dramatic. Be careful to distinguish between being in love with romance and being in love with a person.

———————| Excessive 4 |———————

The tendency is to be obsessive-compulsive about work, too rigid, methodical and structured. Try to relax and have fun.

Excessive 5

May tend to release excess physical energy destructively through physical abuse, temper eruptions, and addictions. Seek constructive outlets for your energy by focusing it on physically demanding work or sports. Try to moderate your cravings for excitement and for sexual extremes. Be careful not to use others just for fun or merely as a stimulant for your own pleasures.

Excessive 6

The tendency is to be enmeshed within family structure to the extent that you cannot stand or think alone. Try not to be overly concerned with status, with pleasing others, or with being the center of attention. Avoid entanglement in others' issues and gossip as you may tend to be perceived as a tattle or blabbermouth.

Excessive 7

The tendency is to be an elitist, bigoted, self-righteous and scornful of others you consider "low-life." Broaden your perspective by learning to accept imperfection in yourself and others. Balance your tendency to focus on the abstract by involving yourself in the practical worlds. Try to relate to and connect with others.

Excessive 8

There may be tendencies to be sadistic, dominant, invasive, jealous, and greedy. Share power and seek consensus with others on issues that are not strictly "black or white," right or wrong. Be careful not to condemn or pass judgment against others too quickly.

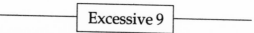

Excessive 9

The tendency is to be the indispensable savior who gives too much and robs others of learning their own lessons. Be careful not to lose yourself in others' needs. Temper your idealism so that you won't get stuck in trying circumstances and give up in despair and martyrdom. Let go of the past—move on.

ACHIEVING BALANCE

Pythagorean numerics suggest certain helpful approaches to healing and the harmonization of imbalances. Here are some of the guiding principles for achieving balance.

▼ Every issue or conflict becomes a focusing lens that magnetizes its own solutions through the convergence of all nine numerical pathways, with their different energies and frequencies. Relieve the particular area of discomfort, pain or emptiness by involving other helpful energies within the spectrum. Keep the dialogue open.

▼ If the problem is ODD, the solution is often EVEN. If the problem is EVEN, the solution is frequently ODD. For example, if there is too much SIXness (enmeshment, family issues), bring in more 5 energy (variety, meeting others, travel) and 7 energy (finding out who you are *alone* in God, inner reflections, study and knowledge).

▼ Begin with the "book end" approach: work toward harmony, resolving the problem by using the energies on each side of the issue. For example, if the problem is too much 4 (workaholic, obsessive-compulsive), relieve it by using 3 (creativity and romance) and 5 (fun, variety, and spontaneity). Then work out toward the full spectrum to relieve the problem area.

▼ Try to find the way of least resistance. Redirect the energy, freeing up blocks and suppressions. Find the true motivation or dream, the deep desire and the need, which together bring fulfillment. Do not focus just on the problem or the surface behavior. Look deeper to the underlying implications. Focus and diversify the energy appropriately. If the problem indicates scatteredness, bring in energies of focus and concentration. If the problem indicates fixations and too much intense concentration, diversify energies toward larger resolutions. Remain expansive, yet focused.

▼ Remember the connectedness of all nine energies interacting. All the numerical energies are related to one another in such a way that each of them involves all the others. A problem is best handled, not just in one way, but through the synthesis and larger balancing of all the nine energy harmonics. Consider various energy combinations (such as 2/8 or 3/5/6 or 1/2/7) as musical chords or *bions* (energy configurations).

▼ Approach life in a spirit of synthesis and inclusivity. What you despise or try to eradicate, forms an attachment and often magnetizes into your life the very person or experience you wish to avoid. Embrace and release lovingly? All lives, at a deep level, are connected!

▼ ODD numerical energies tend to break up existing patterns. EVEN energies tend to stabilize patterns. Learn when and how to use each. Link the potentials of the different numerical energies to your own capacities and predilections:

- Do you prefer to work with people and situations?
- Do you prefer to work with information and data?
- Do you prefer to work with objects and machines?
- Do you prefer to work with Nature?

▼ Remember these basic universal needs:

- Discover and perceive!
- Feel and do!
- Empower with your own power!
- Share and contribute!
- Learn the deeper meaning and significance!
- Bless and love all!

Using Pythagorean numerics, remember life's basic themes:

1 │ Discovering new ideas and possibilities.

2 │ Linking closely.

3 │ Living your dream.

4 │ Achieving the goal through planning and work.

5 │ Experiencing excitement, sensation, and adventure.

6 │ Loving and being loved through friends and social interaction.

7 │ Living out your own meaning and truth.

8 │ Realizing success with empowerment and justice for others.

9 │ Practicing brotherhood and compassionate service to all.

Use creative visualizations to contact the nine pathways of power.

Visualize a clear, fresh-flowing fountain, streaming upward. See the fountain spreading light and vitality; let the bursts of energy flow upward, then feel them cascading down over you, balancing you on the left and right, empowering and centering you now. Describe how you see/view these power streams. Receive new archetypes.

Watch the bird in flight, taking wing in perfect balance, centering inward from right and left, soaring higher, spreading full in the poised stillness of its wings. How do you visualize a particular balance that needs to occur in your life?

Feel the coat of many colors mantling and empowering you with the great energy streams of the universe, as described by numerics.

See the nine power streams as great wheels of power, surrounding you in their spirals and giving you light and strength. What do you see in these wheels, and how are different wheels combining and feeding you?

Feel the streams of a rainbow-waterfall; receive the great reservoirs of electric power, the colorful streams of energy that flow through you now. Receive the vibrations of color energies.

Visualize the great Archai hosts, the great Angels of the cosmos, who empower and direct the nine pathways of power, filling your receptive consciousness with archetypes of possibility. In your meditation, perhaps you will receive new archetypes for your life path. Invoke in the name of the Christ your own guardian Angel's help.

Every time you contact and draw upon the various power pathways, it is like adding new feathers to your headdress. Your aura or energy field expands, expressing more fully the sounds, colors, and tones of Divine mantling, embracing you now.

CONCLUSION

Nobody is just a number! Yet, the nine Pythagorean pathways of power indicate a limitless source of inspiration and energy that is available to all and sparks each individual's deepest personal dreams and motivations. All numbers, as vibrational energies, are potentially beneficial power sources for every person. Our own consciousness and receptivity determine how the energies manifest in our character and behavior.

In my workshops and during my years of university teaching and research, I have found the energies of Pythagorean numerics to be of great value to many students and clients. In counseling, Pythagorean numerics has offered a non-judgmental focus and a spectrum for approaching problems and emotional-psychological-spiritual challenges. Especially helpful for handling difficulties in personal relationships, Pythagorean numerics has provided a clarity and depth that sees through to the essential issues. Whereas other approaches to therapy may often involve much more subjective response, embedded evaluation, and often may take much more time, Pythagorean numerics strikes through to the core of the actual problem and also offers unbiased, creative options for working through discords and achieving greater harmony. I have found Pythagorean numerics to be a very helpful tool in counseling and teaching, and I enjoy sharing it with others who may be able to use it constructively in their own lives and work. When a person can see clearly the nature of a particular problem, or an opportunity for growth, action can be taken more quickly, appropriately, and with more willingness. I believe that along with other helpful therapeutic processes, the Pythagorean perspective of the nine great energy streams of life can certainly facilitate the healing journey and help individuals see more clearly the path they most deeply wish or need to follow. The destiny of every person is unique; Pythagorean numerics honors this uniqueness, and expands the horizons of every sincere seeker.

SUGGESTED READING

Balliett, L. Dow. *Nature's Symphony*. Mokelumne Hill, CA: Health Research, 1968.

_____. *Vibration of Numbers*. London: L. N. Fowler, 1905.

Bullinger, E. W. *Number in Scripture*. London: Lamp Press Ltd., 1952.

Cole, K. C., *Sympathetic Vibrations*. New York: Bantam Books, 1985.

Combs, Allan and Mark Holland. *Synchronicity*. New York: Paragon House, 1990.

Conant, Levi Leonard. *The Number Concept*. New York: MacMillan, 1910.

Curtiss, F. Homer and Harriette. *The Key to the Universe*. New York: E. P. Dutton, 1919.

David, John. *Biblical Numerology*. Grand Rapids, MI: Baker Book House, 1978.

Gibson, Walter. *The Science of Numerology*. New York: George Sully & Company, 1927.

Guthrie, Kenneth Sylvan. *The Pythagorean Sourcebook and Library*. Grand Rapids, MI: Planes Press, 1988.

Johnson, Vera. *The Secrets of Numbers*. New York: Dial Press, 1973.

Jordan, Juno. *Numerology: The Romance of Your Name*. Santa Barbara, CA: J. F. Rowny Press, 1965.

Lingerman, Hal A. *Living Your Destiny*. York Beach, ME: Samuel Weiser Inc., 1992.

Newhouse, Flower A. *Disciplines of the Holy Quest*. Escondido, CA: The Christward Ministry, 1959. The following audio cassettes are available from The Christward Ministry, 20560 Quest Haven Rd., Escondido, CA, 92025.

> "Highlights of the Study of Numbers" (2/2/1958);
>
> "Numbers Have Meaning and Importance" (7/23/1961);
>
> "Numbers and Their Symbolical Content" (10/16/1966);
>
> "The Pythagorean Teaching about Numbers" (9/14/1969);
>
> "The Importance of Your Name" (5/17/1970);
>
> "The Value of Numbers" (2/27/1977);
>
> "The Importance of Names" (3/6/1977).

Oliver, George. *The Pythagorean Triangle*. Minneapolis, MN: Wizards Bookshelf, 1975.

Sinetar, Marsha. *Ordinary People as Monks and Mystics: Lifestyles for Self-Discovery*. Mahwah, NJ: Paulist Press, 1986.

Verny, Thomas. *Nurturing the Unborn Child*. New York: Bantam Doubleday, 1991.

_____. *The Secret Life of the Unborn Child*. New York: Delta, 1988.

Westcott, W. Wynn. *Numbers*. London, England: Theosophical Publications, 1973.

Wilson, Ernest. *You and the Universe*. San Diego, CA: Harmonial Publishers, 1925.

INDEX

Jon Lyons

Hal A. Lingerman is a teacher, ordained minister, and psychological counselor and has worked with various schools, businesses, churches, and other professional groups to help people increase creativity, understanding, and basic life intentions. He is a graduate of Drew and Harvard Universities, as well as Union Theological Seminary and National University in San Diego, California. He holds Masters degrees in Counseling and Psychology, Philosophy/Religion, Russian Language and Literature. He is the author of *Living Your Destiny*, another book about number symbolism, published by Samuel Weiser. In addition he has also published *The Healing Energies of Music, Life Streams*, and *Harmonizing the Classroom*.